BATHROOM BOOK
of
CHRISTMAS TRIVIA

Stories, Weird Facts & Folklore
Behind Holiday Traditions
from Around the World

BATHROOM BOOK
of
CHRISTMAS TRIVIA

Stories, Weird Facts & Folklore
Behind Holiday Traditions
from Around the World

Lisa Wojna

BLUE
BIKE
BOOKS

The Publisher: Blue Bike Books

Library and Archives Canada Cataloguing in Publication

Wojna, Lisa, 1962–
   Bathroom book of Christmas trivia : stories, weird facts & folklore behind holiday traditions from around the world/ Lisa Wojna; illustrator, Roger Garcia.

ISBN-13: 978-1-897278-14-7
ISBN-10: 1-897278-14-4

   1. Christmas—Miscellanea. I. Garcia, Roger, 1976– II. Title.

GT4985.W65 2006   394.2663   C2006-905070-8

Project Director: Nicholle Carrière
Project Editor: Nicholle Carrière
Illustrations: Roger Garcia
Cover Image: Roger Garcia

We acknowledge the support of the Alberta Foundation for the Arts for our publishing program.

PC: P5

DEDICATION

To Jada, the best Christmas present ever. And to all who hold the meaning of Christmas dear—peace on earth and goodwill to all people.

ACKNOWLEDGMENTS

Writing may be a solitary journey, but creating a book never is. This collection of Christmas trivia is no exception.

First and foremost, I'd like to thank Lynne Revill of the Wetaskiwin Public Library. An all-out Christmas enthusiast who is frequently referred to during the festive season as Mrs. Christmas by all the staff there, Lynne dug out a mountain of books—several of them from her own collection—within five minutes of my telling her my next project was a book of Christmas trivia.

Of course, thank you to all the staff of the Wetaskiwin Public Library. They're always great about my ongoing requests and last-minute phone calls begging them to renew my books.

Thank you to Faye, who over the years, and whether she likes it or not, has rapidly moved from the status of my publisher to my mentor and friend. Her unending patience with my neurotic worries is priceless and dear to me.

Thank you to my editor Nicholle. She had the task of editing this copy and the arduous responsibility of making sure each section and subsection and sub-sub-subsection was in just the right order so readers will get the most out of these stories—and she did it all with a smile on her face and constant good cheer.

And, as always, thank you to my family—my husband Garry, my children Peter, Melissa, Matthew and Nathan, and my granddaughter Jada. Without you, all this and anything else I do in my life would be meaningless.

CONTENTS

INTRODUCTION

I remember taking my first course at the University of Manitoba. It was a course in Christian studies, and though I had been a practitioner of the faith for as long as I could remember, I was absolutely blown away by the revelation of how ignorant I really was.

Writing this book has been a lot like that for me.

I love everything Christmas. I sing Christmas carols year round, much to the chagrin of my long-suffering husband. My kids remember me starting my Christmas baking as early as September and October—and loudly lament about those good old days whenever life gets hectic and the scents of cinnamon and ginger don't reveal themselves in my home until December. We've always had an Advent calendar, lit the candles on the Advent wreath at our church and taken part in just about every Christmas season church service and community celebration possible.

But just days into my research for this trivia book, and wow, was I ever humbled once again. After all, I'd never heard of a glass pickle ornament that you hide in the Christmas tree! The Night of the Radishes festival was a complete mystery. And even though I'm part Ukrainian, I found it hard to imagine decorating my Christmas tree with spiderwebs, even if they are supposed to be good luck. I was fast realizing how little I knew about one of my favorite subjects—Christmas!

And so one of my most uplifting writing and research journeys to date began, and a book was born. (I'm such a marshmallow!)

Although I've attempted to touch upon as many different ethnic, religious and secular traditions as possible, this is far from a compete compendium of world Christmas traditions. What I have attempted to do is collect an assortment of odd, inspirational and unusual customs from around the world and mix them with some more commonly known, cherished traditions. I've also delved into the stories behind some of Christmas' favorite and most beloved music, movies and stories.

At the same time, please understand that not every tradition is covered within these pages, nor is this a comprehensive look at every culture or custom. In fact, not all sources agree on the origins or development of many of the customs I've included. Nor are all the legends and stories surrounding the traditions explained here—I've only included the most popular explanation.

These tidbits simply provide a sneak peek into other ways of celebrating the season, and hopefully, as you sift through these pages, you will find a richness and diversity that can only add to your Christmas experience for years to come.

Why December 25?

But the angel said to them, "Do not be afraid. I bring you good news of great joy that will be for all people. Today, in the town of David, a Savior has been born to you; he is Christ the Lord."

– Luke 2:10–11

CHOOSING THE DATE

Winter Solstice and the Celebration of Christmas

Without getting too carried away by the science of the season, the word "solstice" comes from the Latin *sol stitium* and literally means "the sun stands still." The solstice usually occurs on December 21 or 22 for those who reside in the Northern Hemisphere. It is the shortest day of the year and acts as a reminder that the seasons are, once again, changing.

At some point in history, the significance of this seasonal change was noticed and marked as an event worth celebrating. Because of errors in the Julian calendar in use at that time, the winter solstice actually took place on December 25. And during the reign of Roman Emperor Aurelian, sometime in the latter half of the third century, that day was chosen to host a new annual festival the emperor called the "Birth of the Invincible Sun."

Following the birth of Christ and Christianity, and especially once Christianity became Rome's official religion, it seemed a natural thing for scholars and theologians to adopt that day to celebrate the Christmas holiday. After all, most of the civilized world at that time was already accustomed to celebrating on December 25.

Commemorating Christ's birth on the winter solstice—when the world would be graced with increasingly longer periods of light each day for a number of months to come—was somewhat providential in that Christ is often referred to in the Bible as the "Light of the World" or the "Sun of Righteousness."

And so it came to pass that the first time Christmas was celebrated on December 25 was in the year 366 AD, and it has become a tradition that is still upheld by most Christian cultures around the world.

HYVAA JOULUA
in Finnish

The Supper Table

Who doesn't love a great meal?

Unlike every other living creature that shares this planet we call home, for humans, consuming food has never been just about maintaining life—it's about enjoying what we eat!

The elite in ancient Egypt, for example, could choose from as many as 40 different kinds of bread and pastries at their daily supper table, not to mention a huge assortment of dried and fresh fruit, meats and fish. Throughout history, cultures were frequently defined as civilized and a person's status in that culture was often evaluated by what was served at the supper table. And at no other time was the quality of food more important than when celebrating some great event.

So it follows that Christmas—one of the holiest days in the Christian church year—is celebrated in cultures around the world by a grand feast. Even families of modest means attempt to scrape together everything they can to create a special meal to enjoy with their loved ones. That meal has evolved through the ages and from culture to culture, but the value of dining together, especially at Christmas, is as important now as it was when the custom first began.

MAIN COURSES

Khristos Rodyvsya! Christ is Born!

The 12 meatless dishes served on Christmas Eve, which are meant to symbolize the 12 apostles, is the most important part of seasonal food celebrations in Ukrainian homes. Also known as *Sviata Vechera*, or the Holy Supper, the meal is served on a table decorated with wisps of hay to signify Christ's birth in a lowly manger. A sheaf of wheat called the *didukh*, which translated means "grandfather spirit," is often brought to the table by the head of the household to represent the importance of the ancient and rich wheat crops to the Ukrainian people.

Christmas Eve dinner begins with a serving of *kutia*, a pudding-like mixture of boiled wheat, poppy seed and honey. Legend has it that if you take a spoonful of *kutia* and throw it to the ceiling and it sticks, it's a sign of good luck and prosperity for the household.

A typical Ukrainian Christmas feast features delicacies that include *kutia*, borsch (cabbage and beet soup), *holubsti* (rice wrapped in cabbage leaves), jellied fish, poppy seed cakes and *vyrenyky* (more commonly known as perogies).

Phew! I feel full just thinking about it!

DID YOU KNOW?

"Christmas" literally means Christ's Mass and comes from the Old English *Cristes maesse*. And though the actual date of Christ's birthday is unknown, the first birthday celebration—or Christmas—was believed to have taken place in 366 AD.

Mattak

While the name *mattak* sounds interesting, I'm convinced you have to actually be from Greenland to fully appreciate this "delicacy." After the folk from that country have topped off their Christmas feast with coffee, cake and carol singing, a slice of *mattak* is handed to everyone gathered. Hmmm. I bet you're wondering what this delectable treat is. Well, it's said to taste like coconut, but I dare you to give it a try and decide for yourself. Oh, by the way, *mattak* is a slice of whale skin with a layer of blubber attached. Most people can't chew it, so they swallow it whole.

I thought you'd wince!

DID YOU KNOW?

In Greenland, it's customary for the men to wait on the women during the Christmas meal! Sounds good to me—minus the *mattak*, of course.

Please Pass the Emu

Europeans may have made their mark on the wild and mystical country of Australia. And there's no doubt that many Australian Christmas customs—including the traditional festive feast—are strongly influenced by the tastes and preferences of the northern continent. But today, more and more homegrown Australian food is appearing on the family dinner plate, and subsequently, increasingly making a mark on Christmas dinner.

Turkey, ham and plum pudding are seasonal favorites, but so is roast beast—and that might mean anything from char-grilled baby octopus to roasted kangaroo rump or wattleseed crocodile with riberry confit. Of course, cooking on the "barbie" is often seen as the best way to prepare a feast in scorching hot weather. Toss in an assortment of native berries, nuts and herbs, and there's no doubt that Christmas dinner Down Under is an experience unto itself.

Mouth-Watering Filipino Cuisine

For Christmas in the Philippines, specialty rice dishes include delicacies such as the sweet *bibingka* and the purple-blue-colored *puto bumbong*. A chocolate-flavored drink called *tsokolate* and a ginger tea known as *salabat* are seasonal favorites. And for the main course, how about oxtail stewed in peanut butter sauce and pan-fried roast pork, followed by banana fritters and churros for dessert?

The Staff of Life

The festive centerpiece on the table of most Greek homes is called a *Christopsomo* or "Christ bread." It is usually large and round and contains all sorts of interesting ingredients such as dried fruit or nuts. But perhaps the most unique feature of this hearty loaf is that the baker in each household decorates the bread to represent the occupation of the head of the household. For example, the family of a farmer who keeps livestock might have cutout shapes of cows or sheep on the family's bread.

For those families who adhere to fasting during the four weeks before Christmas, it is the father's duty to break that fast with the breaking of the *Christopsomo*. But before dividing the loaf among his family, he blesses it by evoking the Trinity—God the Father, God the Son and God the Holy Spirit. The first portion of bread is reserved for the baby Jesus. Another portion is set aside for the poor and yet another for the house. Then each member of the family is given a share.

Oh, and speaking of farm families, it's not unusual for them to bake loaves shaped in the form of their animals. The Greeks believe that by doing this and then sharing these loaves with their animals, the family would have healthy livestock in the New Year.

A Greek Feast

While you will likely find a roast turkey on a Greek Christmas table, the bird isn't the sole, star attraction it is in a traditional North American household. *Stifado* (beef stew), roast pork flavored with lemon, oregano and rosemary and an avalanche of Greek delicacies follow. For those who have tried it, the spinach-stuffed phyllo pastry known as *spanakopita* is definitely something to look forward to. Then there's *moussaka*, an eggplant and ground beef concoction. But for those of us with a sweet tooth, the pièce de résistance is definitely the *baklava*, a confection of phyllo pastry, honey and walnuts.

DID YOU KNOW?

In the Christmas game "Snap Dragon," which originated in Victorian England, participants try to pick currants out of a bowl of flaming brandy. Ouch!

Something Fishy Here!

Although not prevalent in all parts of the country, preparing vast numbers of fish dishes seems to be traditional in the central and southern parts of Italy. Families may prepare as many as 13 fish dishes for the Christmas Eve meal, and whatever number is chosen is significant in some way to a particular family.

For example, a family may choose to make seven fish dishes to represent the seven days of the week or the seven sacraments of the church. Nine dishes represent the Holy Trinity three times over, and 11 represents the 11 faithful Apostles—Judas is, for obvious reasons, not included. On the other hand, preparing 13 dishes represents all 12 apostles and Jesus. Fishy delicacies can include *calamari* (squid), eels, steak fish and shrimp.

DID YOU  KNOW?

It's commonly believed that the Coca-Cola Company invented the modern image of Santa Claus back in 1931 as a sales gimmick. Not so. At least one source points to an 1885 greeting card created by artist Louis Prang as evidence that Santa was already depicted as a rather rotund, jolly old fellow with a white beard long before Coke's artist Haddon Sundblom drew his famous image of Santa sporting a bottle of Coke in one hand.

NATALE HILARE
in Latin

DESSERTS

The Great Bake-Off!

While the food served at Christmas dinner tables around the world is unique to its country of origin, in Denmark, the tradition around the actual baking of their famous paper-thin spice cookies known as *Brunekage* is a ritual of its very own.

The dough for this Danish delicacy is prepared two or three weeks before baking. This allows the spices to permeate the dough for a more flavorful cookie. Then, on what the Danes call "Baking Day"—usually sometime in mid-December—as many as 400 cookies are produced per household! Talk about being ready for company!

Another unique twist to Christmas dinner in Denmark is that it begins with rice pudding. Inside every batch of this festive favorite is a whole almond, and the family member who is lucky enough to find the almond in his or her portion of the pudding wins a prize!

More than Just Dessert

Have you ever wondered why one Christmas, not that long ago, chocolate letters appeared on the festive food market? Every letter of the alphabet was available as a solid milk chocolate bar. A cool idea, I remember thinking when shopping for my children's stocking stuffers. But it seems the idea wasn't as new as I once thought. It's a common custom in the Netherlands for children to receive a chocolate representing the first letter of their names. And it seems that the Dutch have a few unique food items that come in all shapes and sizes, and that are sometimes handed out in unique ways.

Take marzipan, for example. This baking paste is made of ground, blanched almonds, powdered white sugar, egg whites and salt, and it is often sculpted into a miniature Sinterklaas (Saint Nicholas), one of his elves or other Christmas symbols. Then, after all this hard work and creativity, it's down the hatch with yet another unique Christmas treat.

Sometimes, it's the delivery that's unusual—oh, and the name of the next seasonal sweet treat is a little misleading, too.

When Sinterklaas stops by the houses of Dutch children on the eve of his birthday, December 5, he and his helper, Black Pete, slide down the chimney and proceed to deliver *Pfeffernüsse*, or peppernuts—a candy that despite its name, sometimes does not contain either nuts or pepper. In fact, peppernuts aren't even candy. They're miniature hard, round spice cookies that the holiday duo tosses about the room, and when the youngsters wake up in the morning, they go hunting for peppernuts.

DID YOU KNOW?

Apparently, throwing food during the Christmas season isn't limited to the Dutch tradition of tossing peppernuts. The Irish have also been known to toss and smack food around. In their case, it's a loaf of bread. Strangely enough, in a country that has experienced a massive famine, it's a tradition that makes a lot of sense to the superstitious among us.

There are a number of variations surrounding this Irish New Year's Eve custom. In one case, the husband of the household uses a loaf of bread and strikes the inside of the door three times. As he does this, he recites a chant to banish misfortune and invite happiness into the home for the coming year. Another version has the wife of the household holding the New Year's cake and warning famine "to retire to the country of the Turks." To make sure their animals don't starve in the coming year, a loaf of bread or the New Year's cake is pelted at the barn door.

Sugar Plum Conundrum

Have you ever wondered what a sugar plum was? The sugar plum of "The Night Before Christmas" and other general Christmas folklore was likely the original, sugar-coated coriander treat. Some sources say that though they're not called by this name any longer, a sugar plum is actually a chocolate stuffed with fruit, cream or other sweets. On the other hand, a recipe on the Internet calls for a blending of figs, nuts, honey and spice. The mixture is then formed into balls and rolled in white sugar. Take your pick—they all sound good!

The British Tradition

When most of us hear of mince pies and plum pudding, we automatically think of a good old-fashioned British Christmas feast—and there appears to be a lot of history connected with these holiday staples.

Sources differ as to the origin of plum pudding. According to one legend, one Christmas Eve in the 14th century, an English king and his hunting party found themselves lost in a blizzard. Cold and hungry, and with not much of anything to prepare a meal, they tossed all their rations together—whatever meat they had on hand, fruit, flour, sugar and even a shot or two of brandy—and created a porridge or stew-type of dish that was originally called *frumny*. By 1595, the national dish had evolved into something more like the plum pudding we know today, and it was George I who introduced plum pudding into the Christmas feast back in 1714.

All Things Gingerbread

Soft or hard, thick or thin, cake or cookie—whatever the color or consistency, the scent of baking gingerbread has been around, at least in Europe, since the 11th century.

In the beginning, gingerbread meant "preserved ginger" and was just that—preserved portions of the root eaten like candy. But by the 15th century, the term gingerbread had come to mean a kind of cake made with treacle, a thick syrup that is drained from raw sugar during the refining process, and then flavored with ginger. With a little experimentation, ginger became an ingredient in other types of cakes, as well as in cookies and candy. And almost from the beginning, gingerbread was frequently cut into the shape of people, stars or animals and then colorfully decorated or stamped with a mold and dusted with sugar. The particular season of the year usually dictated what shape was cut. For example, in the spring, gingerbread might be cut into flower shapes.

During Christmas, gingerbread cookies were often cut in the shapes of nativity characters, or perhaps the boy and girl of the Hansel and Gretel story might be cause for inspiration. But a concrete explanation of why the close association between gingerbread men and Christmas has developed seems as elusive as ever. Still, for many of us, the scent of gingerbread is as tied to the Christmas season as is holly, ivy or even the Christmas tree.

DID YOU  KNOW?

Thought to be inspired by the fairy tale of Hansel and Gretel, the tradition of building gingerbread houses is believed to have originated in Germany. Traditionally, a decorated gingerbread house would sit on display throughout the Christmas season, tempting youngsters with its promise of a sweet treat. On New Year's Day, the little gaffers would get to break the house apart and eat the pieces as a formal ushering in of the New Year.

GLEDELIG JU
in Norwegian

Trimming
the Tree

It's hard to imagine Christmas without the image of the family Christmas tree springing to mind. Whether it's green, white or silver, decked out with tinsel and garland or a simple string of popcorn, or elaborately dressed with the finest blown-glass ornaments, the tradition of decorating a Christmas tree is something families around the world participate in.

In our home, the only ornaments that hang on our Christmas tree are handcrafted, and most have some particular significance to our family history. Our two miniature, wooden nutcrackers remind me of when my eldest, in his first school Christmas concert, took part in the musical production of Tchaikovsky's Nutcracker and the Mouse King. *We have a replica of a toy train, painted in a festive green and adorned with an assortment of bright colors, giving it a distinctly Mexican* look. It reminds me of Nana Mouskouri's version of the Christmas carol "Old Toy Trains"—a record I played over and over again until the needle of our old stereo had worn through the vinyl LP.

Throughout the years, my children have contributed some unique, handmade pieces to the tree, taking me back to the days when their eyes were wide with excitement over the season and my biggest concern was making sure they each had a special treat on Christmas morning. Even now, though they are all adults, they pester and prod until the tree is up, usually many days before any of my neighbors.

So as you read about the history of the Christmas tree and the traditions developed by cultures around the world, consider adopting an idea or two for use on your own family tree. Or better still, develop your own unique tree traditions—and hold fast to the memories they produce.

NOT YOUR AVERAGE EVERGREEN

Oh, Christmas Tree!

While the tale of its origin is long and unwieldy, the ritual of decorating a Christmas tree has become almost as revered a tradition in modern times as the reason for the celebration of the season.

Initially, ancient pagans believed the evergreen tree represented the renewal of life because it kept its needles year round. In fact, many ancient traditions worshipped all kinds of trees.

That fact must have been well known
to a seventh-century British monk
named Boniface. He decided to use the natural reverence people already had for this piece of
God's creation in his efforts to bring Christianity to Germany.
According to legend, he was said to have described the Holy
Trinity of God the Father, Son and Holy Spirit using the trian-
gular shape of a fir tree. The lesson worked. Not only did the
German people accept the tenets of the Christian faith, they
continued to honor the fir tree by giving it a special place in the
family home during the Christmas season. It isn't clear why, but
these early Christmas trees were hung upside down from the
ceiling!

It is believed that the first time a Christmas tree was decorated
was in Riga, Latvia, in 1510, using paper flowers. Sources differ
as to how this actually came about. Some say the decorated tree
was "attended by men wearing black hats" and was used for an
annual ceremony that combined both Christian and pagan rituals. The tree was burned as the final part of that ceremony.
Another legend points to a story of religious reformer Martin
Luther, who was said to have decorated a small tree with candles
"to show his children how the stars twinkled through the dark
night."

By the early 1800s, families typically decorated their trees with
fruits and nuts to enhance the evergreen branches. This was said
to represent "the certainty that life would return in the spring."
Once the idea of decorating a family Christmas tree took off,
decorations typically included wax candles, the country's flag,
edible goodies and gifts. Beaded garlands first appeared in
Lauscha, Germany, in the 1850s, but the German innovation
of tinsel didn't arrive on the scene until 1610. And they didn't
spare any expense in its production, either! It wasn't until well
into the second half of the 20th century that the real silver
used in the production of tinsel was replaced with something
less expensive.

Today, the people of Riga have marked the site where they believe the first Christmas tree (also known as a New Year's tree) was erected with an octagonal plaque, which is secured in front of the House of Blackheads. Engraved on each of the eight sides, in eight different languages, are the following words: *The First New Year's Tree in Riga in 1510.*

Worth the Wait

While youngsters in the western world might get the chance to gaze at the twinkling lights and colorful balls of their family Christmas tree for several weeks prior to the big day itself, children in Austria have historically had to wait for that opportunity.

An Austrian Christmas tree is usually fir or pine and is lavishly decorated with gold and silver garlands, an assortment of ornaments and finished off with candles gracing each branch. While the parents may have been busy adding the final touches to the family tree for days, nobody gets to see it until Christmas Eve. That's because it's kept in a locked room, awaiting its formal unveiling.

Tradition dictates that the father of the family reads the story of the Christ child following the Christmas Eve supper. It is only then that the tree is unveiled, with presents spread beneath it, and the family celebrates the season by singing Christmas hymns such as "Stille Nacht" ("Silent Night") and "O Tannenbaum" ("O Christmas Tree").

DID YOU  KNOW?

Before the Christmas tree made an appearance in Canadian homes during the holidays, it was customary for families to hang a "kissing bough." Similar to the tradition of the mistletoe, this custom, which is thought to have migrated to Canada from England, permits those meeting underneath the bough to share a kiss. And that's where the similarity ends. To make a kissing bough, any type of evergreen branch is wrapped around a fairly large wire frame to create a sphere. It is then adorned with a bow, a few ornaments, a piece of fruit and maybe even a candle or two. The end result looks nothing like the traditional sprig of mistletoe. But lovers looking for an excuse to smooch would have found it just as beneficial to have around!

A Christmas Tree, You Say?

Although the idea of having a Christmas tree emerged in England because of German immigrants who brought the tradition with them, it was during the reign of Queen Victoria that the decorating of a family Christmas tree first became popular.

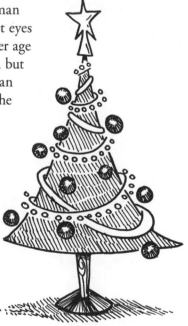

Thanks to an aunt with a German heritage, young Victoria first set eyes on a Christmas tree at the tender age of 13. She was awed, to be sure, but it was years later that her German husband, Prince Albert, made the tradition something the young family looked forward to. In 1848, the *Illustrated London News* publicized the tradition by running an illustration of the Royal Family gathered around their tree. Of course, every patriotic Brit wanted to be like the Royal Family, and there's been no looking back ever since!

Nothing Short of Paradise

The development of the Paradise tree took place in France and coincided with the birth of the Paradise play, the story of Adam and Eve. While the custom of the annual Paradise play died out, the tradition of making a Paradise tree continues in many homes to this day.

In the 15th century, an apple tree bearing apples, meant to represent the Garden of Eden, was simply decorated with Communion wafers. The apples were meant as a reminder of the Adam and Eve story and our earthly beginnings, and the wafers were a reference to the reenactment of the Last Supper during the Holy Eucharist. When an apple tree wasn't available, apples were hung along with the wafers on fir trees or other evergreens. Eventually, pastry ornaments in the shape of stars, hearts, animals, people and other objects made from white or brown dough, depending on the image being represented, replaced the wafers as tree ornaments.

Today, a typical Paradise tree is about eight feet tall and is pruned into topiary with three tiers, each about one foot apart.

The Italian Ceppo

In Italy, a traditional Christmas tree of sorts called a *ceppo* consists of little more than three wooden poles and several shelves arranged in the form of a pyramid. Items such as candy, fruit, presents and decorations are placed on each of the shelves, and a candle is fixed to every corner of each shelf. Most prominently displayed is a handcrafted manger scene—a miniature replica of the nativity scene, complete with an assortment of animals, Wise Men and shepherds, as well as Mary, Joseph and the Christ child.

Pyramid Trees

Although sources differ, it is believed that pyramid trees, also known as Christmas pyramids or *Weinachts pyramide*, were first created by miners living in the Erzgebrige region of Germany. The complexity of a pyramid tree can vary from a simple three-pole variation of the *ceppo* to an elaborately carved, multi-story version often seen on display at public markets in Germany and other European countries. A pyramid tree on public display often has detailed, intricate carvings on every visible piece of wood. Sometimes tree branches and colored paper are also used to add to the decoration. Angels, nativity scenes and other symbolic figurines decorate each level. Even mining processions may be replicated, paying tribute to the tree's origin.

From the pyramid tree's inception, light has always been an important part of the Christmas pyramid and symbolizes a guiding light of sorts that shone brightly, leading miners out of the darkness of the pits to the safety of their homes. Originally, candles were placed on every corner of each tier. Today, electric lights are most often used.

Although Christmas pyramids are typically quite elaborate today, the original three-poled version was known as the "poor man's Christmas tree" and evolved as a substitute Christmas tree for families who couldn't afford a real one.

DID YOU KNOW?

Richard Paul Evans, the author of *The Christmas Box*, used some of his royalties earned through that story to build a shelter for abused children.

The Jesse Tree

A shoot will spring forth from the stump of Jesse, and a branch out of his roots. (Isaiah 11:1)

Simply put, a Jesse tree is a collection of symbols describing the Old Testament story leading up to the birth of Christ, who was prophesied to come from the family of King David, whose father's name was Jesse. It's a family tree of sorts that is typically used in Christian churches to teach children and remind families of certain milestones in the church, beginning with the creation story and continuing through to the birth of Christ. A symbol is used for each story. For example, a dove is used to signify the creation story, a lamb signifies the Passover and Exodus, a white lily represents the hope promised through Mary's story and a chi (X) rho (P)—a symbol made up of these two Greek letters superimposed on top of one another—is used to signify the Son of God. A custom of some Christian churches is to celebrate each Sunday of Advent, which is the period of four weeks before Christmas, by adding another seven symbols to their Jesse tree, which is likely proudly perched at the front of the church, to signify the seven lessons of each week.

The Chrismon Tree

Unlike its cousin the Jesse tree, the focus behind the Chrismon tree is entirely on all things related to Christ and the Christmas story. As the name itself suggests, the Latin word *chrismon* relates to monograms or symbols representing the "nature and character of Jesus." There are many dozen chrismons, and I certainly couldn't find any source that would confine itself to a single number figure, but some of the more common chrismons include a variety of crosses, the chi rho (also used in the Jesse tree), a triangle with a circle woven through its sides, a crown of thorns with the image of three nails inserted through it, an eight-pointed star (representing the eight knightly virtues of tact, perseverance, gallantry, loyalty, dexterity, explicitness,

observation and sympathy), the eternity symbol of a sideways figure-eight and many others. Most often, these chrismons are made from paper. But some are more elaborate, being made into a three-dimensional ornament or cross-stitched on fine Aida cloth and placed inside miniature frames. Either way, the Chrismon and Jesse trees are wonderful examples of ways to stay focused on the Christmas story.

DID YOU KNOW?

The word "mistletoe" is an Anglo-Saxon word meaning "dung on a twig." Apparently, the name came from the fact that in ancient times it was thought "life could spring spontaneously from dung." Mistletoe grows on tree branches, and since bird droppings are commonly found on tree limbs, or so it was thought, the words *mistle*, meaning "dung," and *tan*, meaning "twig," were blended to form the word mistletoe or "dung on a twig."

A Christmas Tree for the Nation

It was back in 1923 when U.S. President Calvin Coolidge lit the first "National Community Christmas Tree" in Washington, D.C. The 48-foot-high balsam fir was cut and shipped from Coolidge's home state of Vermont and presented by Paul D. Moody. That first tree shone like no other, decked out in 2500 red, white and green Christmas lights, and started an annual tradition that continues to this day.

The pressure was on for a vital, growing nation to celebrate Christmas with a living tree, and a 35-foot-high Norway spruce was obtained from a nursery in New York and donated by the American Forestry Association. That tree was planted at Sherman Plaza, at the east entrance to the White House. The tradition of using a living tree for the Christmas celebration in the nation's capital continued for some time, though the location of the tree moved from Sherman Plaza (1924–33) to Lafayette Park (1934–38) and back to President's Park, now known as the Ellipse, in 1939. Regardless of the location, live trees were used until 1954, when cut trees were reintroduced. Live trees returned as the nation's Christmas tree in 1973 and continue to be used to the present day.

Building on the theme of peace on earth and goodwill to all, the first "Christmas Pageant of Peace," a brainstorm idea of the Washington Board of Trade and the Washington Citizen's Committee, was added to the festivities in 1954 and remains part of the nationwide annual event.

FRÖHLICHE WEIHNACHTEN
in German

Here Comes Santa Claus

As a youngster, I never had the opportunity to partake of an annual visit to a shopping mall Santa. So when my babies were born, I dutifully marched them over to the lap of the nearest Santa I could find and insisted on a picture.

Now, my children weren't always on the same page when it came to this parent-imposed custom, and I have the odd photo of a screaming toddler with arms reaching out, ramrod straight, demanding to be set free from the confines of that funny-looking man's lap to prove it!

Still, the children always left out a snack of milk and cookies on Christmas Eve, just in case this Santa stuff was for real. And there was always a customary letter to Santa—just to be sure he had their Christmas wish list.

Regardless of whether your personal traditions include Santa or not, the story behind this mythical personality, and the spirit in which it was intended, is one that certainly captures the spirit of Christmas.

GOOD DEEDS AND GIFTS

Jolly Old Saint Nicholas

Although the descriptors "jolly" and "old" are recent tags to Saint Nicholas' name, they are qualities that this forerunner to Santa Claus more than likely possessed.

Born in 280 AD, the man who would become Saint Nicholas spent the majority of his life in the area of present-day Turkey. Known as Nicholas, Bishop of Myra, he was a kind and generous man, giving all he had to the poor and needy. One particularly popular story centers around his providing a dowry for three impoverished sisters.

It was widely believed that Nicholas could perform miracles. He was said to have breathed life into dead children, calmed a storm to save three endangered sailors and saved the life of a prisoner sentenced to death.

Needless to say, the bishop was popular in his day, and that popularity continued after his death. Although he was buried in Myra around 340 AD, his body was believed to have been stolen and moved to Bari, Italy, by a group of Italian sailors in 1087.

The church obviously agreed that Nicholas deserved the favor he received from the faithful, and upon his death, promptly canonized him. That, in turn, led to various groups and countries adopting him as their patron saint—children, travelers, sailors and lawyers, to name a few. The Russians depicted him as a wise-looking man with a long, white beard and a red cape and lovingly referred to him as "Miracle Maker."

How Saint Nicholas came to be so intricately tied to Christmas is quite simple, really. When Nicholas was made a saint, his birthday—December 6—was named his feast day. Because it was so close to Christmas and because of his love for children and his generosity, his association with Christmas was a natural fit. In Holland, Sint Nikolaas (later Sinterklaas) Day was the day for gift giving, and Christmas focused solely on the Christmas story and formal worship.

When it comes to his appearance, artistic license has had considerable leeway, thanks in part to Clement C. Moore and his 1822 poem "The Night Before Christmas":

> *He had a broad face and a little round belly,*
> *That shook when he laughed, like a bowl full of jelly,*
> *He was chubby and plump, a right jolly old elf,*
> *And I laughed when I saw him, in spite of myself.*

DID YOU KNOW?

Is nothing what it seems? According to a story in the *New York Times* in 2000, there is some academic speculation as to whether or not Clement Moore actually penned "The Night Before Christmas." Apparently, the "spirit and style" of this Christmas favorite are "starkly at odds with the body of Moore's other writings," Vassar professor Don Foster is quoted as saying. Instead, he suggests that Henry Livingston Jr. is the author and that the original name of the poem was "A Visit from Saint Nicholas."

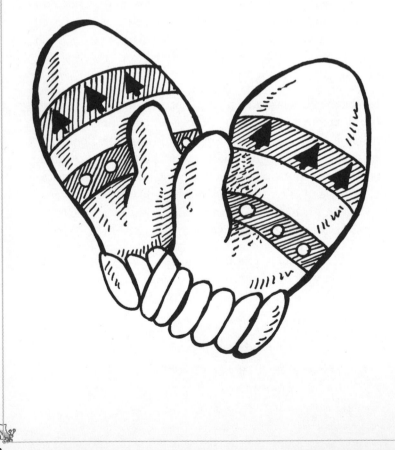

Knecht Ruprecht
and Other Ghoulish Creatures

Concerned their children would receive Christmas gifts indiscriminately regardless whether they'd been good and deserved them or not, German parents developed the tradition of Knecht Ruprecht. While his name, which means "Farmhand Ruprecht" or "Servant Ruprecht," brings forth images of a helper with a kind and loving temperament, everything about this frightening, devilish-looking creature was in direct opposition to what Saint Nicholas stood for. Still, he had a valuable role to play when it came to teaching youngsters the importance of appropriate behavior. Knecht Ruprecht would accompany Santa Claus on his Christmas visits, and it was his job to decide if the children of each household had been good throughout the year and were worthy of receiving a gift. A sure sign that you needed to improve your behavior was waking up to a lump of coal instead of candy, nuts or fruit.

It appears that parents in Germany weren't the only ones with this unique way of handling their naughty offspring. In Holland, Zwarte Piet, or Black Peter, gives Santa a hand in a similar role. And since his name was the same one used to refer to the Devil himself in the Middle Ages, he was a particularly scary creature.

If youngsters in Germany and Holland thought they had it tough, Christmas Eve and the promise of a visit from the Devil must have had children in the Czech Republic and Slovakia hiding under their blankets and shivering from more than just the cold, winter weather. In these countries, the Devil is Saint Nicholas' helper. A shaggy, furry creature with horns, a tail and a long, red tongue that he flicks about in glee, the demon waits for the chance to use his staff to wield a hearty punishment on children who were less than well behaved that year.

A similar type of "helper" appears in a number of ethnic traditions, and each is known by a slightly different name:

🔔 Krampus in Austria and Bavaria, Germany

🔔 Klaubauf in Bavaria, Germany

🔔 Bartel in Styria, Austria

🔔 Pelzbock, Pelznickel, Belsnickel in Pennsylvania

🔔 Schmutzli in Switzerland

🔔 Rumpelklas, Bellzebub, Hans Muff, Drapp, Buzebergt in Augsburg, Germany

🔔 Pére Fouttard in northern France

DID YOU KNOW?

The annual marathon known as Corrida de Sao Silvestre—Saint Sylvester's Race—has been held in downtown Sao Paulo, Brazil, every New Year's Eve since 1924. Initially, the race began the exact moment the clock struck midnight on New Year's Eve. Today, it is held in the afternoon—a change that wasn't welcomed by all Brazilians. The national race went international in 1945, and today, thousands of people take part in the event.

Balthazar

Santa gets a break when it comes to visiting youngsters in Spain, since Christmas tradition in that country doesn't recognize the jolly old elf. Instead, Christmas in Spain remains more focused on religious customs.

Children in that country shouldn't despair, though. A Wise Man named Balthazar visits every home, and children who remember to place their shoes on the windowsill will wake to something special placed inside.

Befana

Christmas celebrations in Italy don't even have a Santa Claus figure. Instead, children there have to wait until the Eve of Epiphany, January 6, to hang stockings for Befana, hoping she will find it in her heart to fill them with goodies.

Befana is a far cry from the jolly figure of Santa. Instead, she's said to be a woman with "a stern nature and forbidding appearance." Her story is a sad one for a Christmas tale. Folklore has it that the three Wise Men happened to pass by Befana's home in search of Bethlehem and the promised Christ child, asking for directions. She pointed the way, but continued with her household chores rather than accompanying the Wise Men,

who were kind enough to ask her along. When a shepherd
stopped a little while later, also asking for directions, Befana
was happy to oblige. Still, her work beckoned her, and she again
declined the offer to travel to the site of the first Christmas
nativity. But when the heavens exploded with the angelic chorus
singing "Glory to God in the highest, and on earth peace,
goodwill towards men," she realized her housework could wait
and hurried to Bethlehem, only to find a vacant stable. By the
time she arrived, the Holy Family had moved on, as had the
Wise Men, shepherds and angels alike. She'd missed the most
important event in history! Still hoping to find the baby Jesus,
Befana was said to have given every child she met a treat, hoping
Jesus was among them.

Her quest was unsuccessful, and to this day, the distraught Befana is believed to wander the hillsides of Italy every year on the Eve of Epiphany—the date that the Wise Men are thought to have visited the Christ child—bringing gifts to children. Naughty youngsters better beware, though. All they receive is a lump of coal.

DID YOU KNOW?

Forget writing a letter, kids in Scotland have to "cry up the lum"—holler up the chimney—with their Christmas gift wishes if they want Santa to get it right on Christmas morning.

Babouschka

No, this isn't the kerchief that women of the Old Country used to wear on their heads. According to Russian legend, Babouschka is a poor, little, crooked, wrinkled, old woman who spends Christmas wandering from house to house searching for the baby Jesus. While she scurries about quite hurriedly throughout the Christmas season, she slows down enough on Christmas Eve to deliver small gifts to little children. Like Befana of Italy, Babouschka is the Santa figure in Russian folklore.

One Hot Christmas
While much of the world is glad to be in from the cold and enjoying Christmas with a cup of hot chocolate, our neighbors to the far south have a much different idea of seasonal festivities. Camping, picnicking and sailing are all commonplace in countries such as Brazil. Yet despite the warm temperatures, which can soar as high as 100°F, Santa Claus—or Papai Noel—still arrives in that country dressed in his customary red and white suit complete with boots black as soot, even though there aren't a lot of chimneys to sail down.

It's not surprising that Santa Claus is the star of the show. His reindeer get a break when Santa travels to the southern climes of Rio de Janeiro. And instead of his usual entourage, Santa is flown in by helicopter and descends on a specially built platform in that city's largest venue—the Marcana Stadium. Although there are quite literally thousands of children clamoring for his attention, each one gets a balloon or water pistol or some other small toy, and then Santa proceeds to lead the crowd in a round of Christmas carols. The scene is repeated in cities throughout Brazil, and each time, Santa touches down in his very own chauffeured helicopter.

FELIZ NAVIDAD
in Spanish

Christmas Around the World

I learned what a narrow view of life I had in 1994, when my family and I moved from the windy prairies of Manitoba to the wilds of northern British Columbia.

Talk about culture shock! Everything was so different. Even my church of choice had different ways of doing things from its counterparts to the east. Although I hadn't left Canada, I still felt like a foreigner.

That the physical and social geography of where we live has a huge part in molding us was never so apparent. So it is with tradition, and regional traditions surrounding Christmas are no exception. What kind of food is placed on the festive table depends on what's available in any one location.

Cultural traditions are often grounded in pre-Christian beliefs, and these spill out into the way Christmas is celebrated in any one community. Even carols imported from other countries take on a new, ethnic flare. Learning about these various customs and the beliefs from which they stem has left me with an even deeper appreciation for this special season.

THE HOLY LAND

A Holy, Holy Christmas

If you're able to travel and have a yearning to experience
a Christmas rich with history, a trip to Bethlehem, in the heart
of the Holy Land, is definitely in order. Built in 325 AD by
Constantine, the first Christian emperor of the Roman Empire,
the Church of the Nativity in Bethlehem is believed to be situ-
ated on the exact spot of Christ's birth. That structure burned
down during a rebellion in 529 AD and was rebuilt shortly after,
making it one of the oldest continuously operating churches in
the world and the only surviving major church in the Holy Land
from the early Christian period. Today, an archbishop of the
Eastern Orthodox Church conducts Christmas services there.

Another tradition unique to Bethlehem is that of the shepherd's field. Thousands of pilgrims travel to a field outside of Bethlehem where it is thought the shepherds of the Christmas story heard the angel proclaiming the birth of Christ. Both major Christian denominations—the Eastern Orthodox and Roman Catholic churches—apparently have rival fields.

DID YOU KNOW?

It appears that a roasted boar's head used to be the Christmas feast of choice in England during the Middle Ages. The most pervasive legend behind the origin of this festive practice has to do with a university student at Oxford's Queen's College. The story goes that the young man was attacked by a wild boar and his only weapon of defense was a copy of the writings of Aristotle. He saved himself from a bitter end by shoving the book down the boar's throat. Of course, the boar died, but the student wasn't satisfied with merely having saved himself. He wanted to save his book as well, so it was off with the boar's head! With book in one hand and boar's head in the other, the lad made his way back to his college, where it is believed all feasted on wild boar that Christmas—and apparently for many Christmases to come!

NORTH AND SOUTH AMERICA

American Festivities

Christmas festivities in the U.S. don't typically begin just a week or two before December 25. In fact, most Americans are gearing up by mid-November. By then, preparations for Thanksgiving, which some may argue rivals Christmas as the most important holiday of the year in that country, are well underway and plans for family get-togethers are being ironed out.

Thanksgiving in the States takes place on the fourth Thursday in November. According to one 19th-century tradition, its origin dates back to 1621, with the first Thanksgiving celebrations held by a group of "separatists from the Church of England" at Plymouth Plantation, Massachusetts. Having landed there the previous year, the group of new settlers joined members of the Wampanoag tribe for a three-day celebration once that year's harvest had been collected. While this is often thought of as the first Thanksgiving celebration, it wasn't until 1623 that the new tradition took on significant religious meaning.

At the same time, other sources point to several Thanksgiving-type feasts or celebrations not connected with harvest time as the being the first of their kind.

- The expedition team led by FranciscoVasquez de Cornado and a group of Native Americans he referred to as the Tejas were believed to have gathered for a feast on May 23, 1541, in Palo Duro Canyon, Texas. In particular, the expedition crew was believed to be giving thanks for food discovered after their supplies ran low.

🔔 On September 8, 1565, explorer Pedro Menedez de Aviles and his crew were said to have feasted with Native Americans at St. Augustine, Florida.

🔔 More than 30 years later, on April 30, 1598, Don Juan de Onate and his men celebrated a feast of thanksgiving with the Manso tribe in Texas.

Still, it appears the annual tradition of celebrating a formal, religious Thanksgiving can indeed be credited back to the Plymouth story. And since 1924, the Macy's Thanksgiving Day Parade, which is held the Wednesday evening before Thanksgiving, has kicked off seasonal celebrations in Midtown Manhattan. Originally organized by Macy's staff, many of whom were second-generation immigrants, the parade has grown to such an extent that it attracts thousands upon thousands of spectators lining city streets and garners a huge television audience throughout Canada and the U.S.

DID YOU KNOW?

Canadians can credit English explorer Martin Frobisher with having held the first Thanksgiving celebration on Canadian soil. As he and his crew were steadfastly working to discover the Northwest Passage, they paused long enough to hold a thanksgiving feast on Newfoundland soil in 1578.

Christmas in Canada

While it's quite obvious that Christmas traditions take on the flavor of the different ethnic traditions of a country, one can't really define a typically Canadian Christmas. The reasons are twofold. First, Canada was founded by First Nations peoples and immigrants from countries around the world. It's also a massive country that spans almost 4,000,000 square miles, so geography often dictates regional traditions. Here are just a few typical activities folk take part in as part of their Christmas traditions:

🔔 The lobster fishing season occurs just before Christmas, so if you live on Prince Edward Island, chances are that a lobster feast will be part of your festive celebrations.

🔔 A French Canadian Christmas might include feasting on voyageur stew, split pea soup or a meat-filled *tourtière* (pork pie), followed by enough traditional dancing to wear off any excess calories accumulated.

🔔 Christmas in the Rockies means all the usual fanfare, plus a round of skiing. Folk who aren't into hitting the slopes, are likely to appreciate the scenery from afar while trekking along a local walking path.

A One-Room Wonder

There aren't many left, but even the remnants of a one-room prairie schoolhouse still bring back a plethora of fond memories for the folks who went to school in them. And most often, the annual Christmas concert tops the list.

Typically, preparations for the annual pageant would begin as soon as fall harvest was completed and youngsters had returned to school. By then, the harried pace of the summer had, for the most part, settled down, and families could direct at least some of their attention away from putting up preserves for the winter months ahead to planning for the coming Christmas season. While youngsters were busy in the classroom, learning their lessons alongside their lines for that year's rendition of the Christmas story, mothers were busy combing through family recipes and collecting ingredients for their family's favorite treats.

Because the annual Christmas concert drew families from miles around, even families who didn't have children in school, the

local community hall had to be transformed into a vision of seasonal perfection in order to accommodate such a big event. In whatever spare time they might steal from one chore or another, community members banded together to clean and decorate the hall. At the same time, youngsters were busy creating handcrafted decorations for the community Christmas tree, while their fathers were out scouting for the perfect specimen. That way, even if Old Man Winter dumped a load or two of snow in the meantime, which sometimes had the effect of making a rather dowdy-looking tree appear more spectacular, the men of the community had already made their choice.

Even though the community hall could be located in the middle of nowhere, on the night of the big event, parking was always at a premium. The night usually began with a round of caroling, followed by the Christmas play and, as with any good community event, a table laden with festive treats. It was a concrete sign that Christmas had arrived, and as people filed out of the building, their faces aglow, snowflakes wafting gently to the ground, for a moment anyway, there was indeed peace in their corner of the earth and goodwill to all in their community.

DID YOU  KNOW?

The word "carol" literally translated means "song of you," and the tradition of singing Christmas carols appears to be of British origin. It is believed that people first began traveling door to door singing carols in the Middle Ages as a gift of Christmas cheer for their family and friends.

A First Nations Christmas

The meaning behind and the traditions around Christmas were introduced to Canada's First Nations people by European settlers. Still, it makes sense that a culture of people with such a strong connection to nature would have established some form of tradition around the winter solstice. Feasting, singing, dancing and drumming were all part of their annual celebrations, along with racing and strength competitions. In some aboriginal cultures, a tobacco ceremony is conducted, and the Creator is asked for a blessing on the coming year's crops.

Today, for First Nations peoples who take part in Christmas, many of these traditions are blended into religious celebrations adopted from European cultures. For example, a large portion of the Mi'kmaq of Nova Scotia adhere to the Christian tradition of caroling and attending church services. Then, in keeping with their own culture, Christmas Eve often ends with a traditional dance.

North to Nunavut

For the Inuit of Canada's north, Christmas means all the usual festivities with a few cultural additions to enrich the season even more. Competitions showcasing traditional skills such as harpoon throwing, whip cracking, wrestling and igloo building are typically held during seasonal celebrations. Games such as the "one-hand reach"—a test of skill in which a man balances his entire body weight on one hand while reaching up with the other to grab a piece of seal meat suspended in the air—are held in Inuit communities throughout the North. While the one-hand reach is a competition reserved for men only, the "good woman contest" is strictly for women. In Inuit culture, a woman's mettle is measured by how well she skins a seal or bakes bannock, which are all part of the contest. At the end of these events, a drum dance is usually held, accompanied by traditional story-telling and throat singing, also known as overtone singing— a unique way of vocalizing in which two women face each other in a friendly competition, alternating throat vibrations in an effort to "imitate sounds of the North." The tones of both woman complement one other. Today, it's common to hear youngsters bebopping, which more than likely stems from this kind of traditional overtone singing.

Another tradition unique to the Inuit is that of *pallaq*, "the running," which is when herds of caribou run. This usually takes place on Boxing Day or New Year's Eve and is followed by another unique celebration. To share their good fortune, one or two members of any family with a particularly good reason to celebrate—and likely most families have something to be excited about—gather clothing, blankets, candies or other items and toss them off the roof of their home to people who gather below.

DID YOU KNOW?

Aussies really know how to make Christmas last for more than just the traditional 12 days. While family preparations might start the month before, formal festivities begin an entire week ahead of the big day. Known as "Run-up to Christmas," Aussies use their warm southern weather to their advantage, hosting numerous parades, festivals and other celebratory events.

Night of the Radishes

Culinary connoisseurs might find this story something they can really sink their teeth into.

In the Mexican city of Oaxaca, December 23 is set aside each year for a rather unique exhibition. And from where I sit, to pull this thing off you need perfect growing weather, some mighty amazing gardeners, crafty carvers and a wild imagination.

The evening is called *Noche de Rábanos* or "Night of the Radishes," and you guessed it—radishes play a pretty prominent role in this event. The biggest and the best are chosen by radish artists throughout the area. Their goal is to carve the best Christmas scene they can in these gourd-sized vegetables. And when I say gourd-sized, I'm not kidding! Some of these radishes weigh in at nearly 10 pounds and measure more than 2 feet in length!

Like their carving counterparts in the stone and wood arena, radish carvers typically look for unique shapes and strong forms that suggest their finished image. For example, a stray bit of root on one radish might work well as a mustache on a bull rider. Another radish might suggest the elegant dress of a dancing girl. Either way, carvers tackle their choice radish three days before the festival, creating scenes that either depict some form of everyday Oaxacan life or a nativity scene, complete with the Holy Family, Wise Men and all.

Although it's unclear if this is the actual origin of the Night of the Radishes, one story tells of how marketplace vendors on Christmas Eve, in an effort to highlight their goods, carved vegetables to attract attention. It is, however, confirmed that the mayor of Oaxaca opened the first exhibition in 1897.

While the festival boasts everything from delicious food and other handcrafted attractions to an elaborate fireworks display, it is the radishes that make this a truly unique event.

DID YOU KNOW?

Christmas Day isn't a festive time for everyone. Charlie Chaplin (1977), Dean Martin (1995) and Jon Benet Ramsey (1996) all died on December 25.

Act One, Scene One

Since the 1980s, Brazilians in Rio de Janeiro have taken to a relatively new tradition—the *Auto de Natal*, or the "Act of Christmas," an outdoor reenactment of the Christmas story. Usually held in the Arcos da Lapa theatre, the annual play— free to all who want to attend—draws large crowds and ensures that even the poorest of the poor can join in celebrating the birth of Christ.

Misa de Gallo, the Rooster's Mass

While celestial angels were the first heavenly beings to announce the birth of Christ, people of the Spanish- and Portuguese-speaking world credit the humble rooster as being the first earthly creature to do so. According to legend, there were actually two roosters involved. In a human voice, the first said: "Christ is born." The second echoed: "In Bethlehem!" Some credit this legend with originating the custom of Midnight Mass. And it is certainly because of the rooster legend that the *Misa de Gallo,* or Rooster's Mass, is one of three Christmas masses celebrated in Roman Catholic churches in these countries.

DID YOU KNOW?

While laws are typically restrictive, Brazil has one law that's particularly attractive when it comes to Christmas festivities. In that country, employers are mandated by the government to provide their employees with a 13th salary, the equivalent of a 13th month of work, to be paid out each year on December 20. The purpose of this extra pay is to help families enjoy the season with a few extras they otherwise likely couldn't afford. Employees who haven't worked with the company for an entire year still receive a 13th salary, but it is prorated to their hours of service.

MERI KIRIHIMETE
in Maori

THE UNITED KINGDOM AND IRELAND

Green Christmas

"A green Christmas makes a fat churchyard." This old Irish saying warns that no snow on Christmas is bad luck. In fact, the aura of death is in the air if you adhere to Irish superstition. On the other hand, snow is a good sign. A "thin churchyard" is predicted, along with a fat goose for Christmas dinner.

Superstitions aside, the Irish enjoy a wide array of Christmas customs, such as the telling of stories on Christmas Eve. These stories might begin with gathering around a peat fire and a retelling of the Christmas story, but they don't end there. They continue on with stories of Irish history, the Great Famine and family memories. Known for their folklore, storytelling is one way the Irish keep their history alive.

DID YOU  KNOW?

The Saturday before Christmas is traditionally known as the "day to bring home the Christmas" in Ireland. Customarily, it's the day families go to market to purchase a goose or turkey—for the more than 40 percent of the population that lives in the rural countryside that goose or turkey is most often a live one—and all the fixings for a "good and proper" Christmas feast.

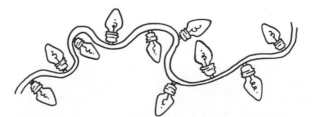

Jolly Old England

What does it mean to "come a-wassailing," anyway? The simple answer is that it's a form of door-to-door caroling in which carolers wish their neighbors good health, which is what the Saxon word *wassail* means. In exchange, the carolers would be given food and drink. But sources differ as to the origin and the reasons behind the custom.

According to some authorities, the practice of wassailing has its roots in the Middle Ages, when a reciprocal hymn was shared between peasants and their feudal lords. Following their gift of the goodwill carol, the peasants would be sent on their way with food and drink and a blessing, of sorts, from the lord of the manor:

> *Love and joy come to you,*
> *And to you your wassail, too;*
> *And God bless you and send you*
> *A Happy New Year.*

Other sources tie the tradition of wassailing to ancient pagan rituals that initiated the practice to "awake the cider apple trees and to scare away evil spirits to ensure a good harvest of fruit in the Autumn." In this case, going wassailing usually occurred on January 6 or 17 (depending on whether you were using the Gregorian or Julian calendar) as a Twelfth Night celebration.

Regardless of its origin—and its evolution through the centuries—going wassailing is practiced in different forms in countries throughout the world to this day.

Christmas in Disguise

Feasting, family, friends and, of course, Midnight Mass, are all part of the seasonal celebrations in many countries around the world. But so is the unique tradition of mumming, also known as mummering.

The word "mummer" literally means "masker." It refers to individuals who dress up in outlandish costumes that completely disguise who they are and go about making merry. It is thought that this strange tradition has its roots in ancient Rome in a festival held in honor of the god Saturn, which usually took place around mid-December.

In the 16th and 17th centuries, mumming consisted of dramatic plays and was commonly practiced in England and Germany during their Christmas celebrations. The practice of mummery and its elaborate folk dramas spread to Scotland, Wales and Ireland in the 17th century and continues to this day. Philadelphia seems to be the mummery hotspot in the United States. Mummery here has evolved to take on a variety of ethnic flavors and is something that state is quite proud of. They even have a Mummer's Museum, and a Mummers Parade is held every New Year's Day.

In Canada, the men and women of the Rock—otherwise known as the province of Newfoundland and Labrador—take to dressing in each other's clothes during the Christmas season and wandering door to door, hoping to be asked in for a glass or two of good cheer.

GLAEDIG JUL
in Danish

SCANDINAVIA

My Own Elf?

Imagine this. You're a little girl, not yet afraid of monsters, when you learn of an elf-like creature that lives in your attic, just waiting for you to make a mistake so he can cast a curse on you and your family! In days gone by, members of Danish households would climb the stairs to their attic just before Christmas and place a bowl of rice porridge to appease this mythological creature known as the *nisse*. Most times, when a family member later went to retrieve the bowl, it was empty. Then everyone would breathe easier, thinking their *nisse* was content with their offering of his favorite food, when in reality, the porridge had likely been consumed by mice!

Rauhallista Joulua, Peaceful Christmas

In Finland, Christmas celebrations officially begin at high noon on Christmas Eve. That's when the Turku city clerk goes on national radio and television to announce a nationwide declaration of peace. A formal Christmas message is read and concludes with the Finnish greeting *Rauhallista Joulua,* which means "peaceful Christmas." It appears this custom has its roots in pre-Christian times, when as many as 27 different times of peace were declared throughout the course of the year.

That a number of pre-Christian traditions have melded with Christian ones is quite evident in Finland. The belief that cleanliness was next to godliness seems to be prevalent in many countries where housecleaning preparations mean more than just sweeping out the cobwebs. In the past, some cultures believed dirt was a gateway for evil spirits to enter a home.

 In Finland, the tradition of cleanliness extends to a centuries-old ceremonial custom in which everyone either visits a public sauna or has a sauna in their private bathhouse. Either way, nobody partakes of Christmas Eve dinner until the entire family has been appropriately cleansed and then dressed in their seasonal finery.

For some Finnish families, there's an additional hurdle to cross before they get to eat Christmas Eve dinner. For these families, a sheaf of grain is attached to a pole. Nuts and seeds are abundantly sprinkled on top of the grain, and the family will not have dinner until the birds have eaten their fill. While there are several variations of this tradition, its origin is a mystery. Perhaps this is an example of the combining of some of the ancient pagan traditions of this country with the more modern-day Christian ones.

In the Christian church, Christmas is commonly referred to as the "Season of Light." The Finnish people act out this belief in a most moving way. On Christmas Eve, the seasonal traditions include a rather solemn act. At nightfall, families place a lighted candle on the graves of deceased family members or friends. The custom extends to the graves of soldiers, the lit candles symbolizing a moving from darkness to light.

DID YOU  KNOW?

For most of the 20th century—from the depths of the Russian Revolution in 1917 until 1992—Christmas and religious traditions of any kind were banned in Russia.

A Swedish Remembrance

The Christmas season in Sweden begins with Saint Lucia Day on December 13 and lasts a full month until the celebration of Saint Knut's Day on January 13.

Saint Lucia Day

The story of Lucia is a sad one, indeed. Legend has it that Lucia was actually of Italian birth and was expected to marry a man she didn't love—a pagan man who didn't share her Christian beliefs. On the eve of her wedding day, she opted to give her dowry to the poor, wanting to remain a virgin. In some variations, her betrothed becomes so angry, he disfigures his wife-to-be, only to have her transform before his eyes into an angelic beauty before she dies. In other variations, it was her actual conversion to Christianity at a time when the faith wasn't accepted in

Rome that caused her to be burned at the stake on December 13, 304 AD. Either way, as is often the case in situations where a person is so misunderstood, Lucia was later seen as a maiden of selfless giving who had great love for those less fortunate. In fact, her love was so profound that one story credits her spirit with having provided food to an entire population severely hit by famine in the province of Varmland, Sweden, during the Middle Ages. She was eventually canonized by the Catholic Church.

In Sweden, the custom of recognizing Lucia on her feast day, December 13, is a family affair in which the eldest daughter dresses in a long, flowing, white robe with a red sash and a crown of nine candles, taking on the role of Lucia. She is the first to rise in the home and is responsible for preparing that morning's meal. She then moves from room to room, all the while singing the Sicilian chorus known as "Santa Lucia" as she makes her way through the house, serving each family member breakfast in bed. The custom of celebrating Saint Lucia Day has developed into an event in which young girls throughout a community compete for the title of the most outstanding Lucia of the season.

Perhaps one of the strangest components to the Saint Lucia Day tradition in Sweden is that though there are lots of suppositions, no one really knows how a saint of Italian origin became such an important part of Swedish tradition.

DID YOU KNOW?

Brazilians take no chances when it comes to ensuring their prosperity for the coming year. Apparently, in that country, eating lentils at the precise moment the clock strikes midnight should bring good fortune.

Saint Knut's Day

King Knut (or Canute IV) of Denmark ruled that country from 1080 to 1086. Also known as a kind and generous human being, King Knut thought extending the Christmas celebrations 20 days after Christmas was the way to go. He was later canonized, and a day was named in his honor. To this day, most of Sweden celebrates the end of the Christmas season on Saint Knut's Day, January 13, with a final tree lighting, followed by the stripping and dismantling of the Christmas tree. Everyone gathers to sing a song in honor of the season and King Knut:

After twenty days on Knut,
We dance the Christmas tree out.

How this tradition from a Danish king was adopted by the Swedish is a matter of history. Denmark, Norway and Sweden were all part of the Kalmar Union and were ruled by a single monarch from 1397 until 1521. Sweden left the union in the early 16th century, but the tradition of Saint Knut's Day remained an important part of Swedish Christmas celebrations.

Buone Natale
in Italian

WESTERN EUROPE

Reliving the Nativity

Although nativity paintings and drawings were already common at the time, Francis of Assisi was credited with developing the concept of replicating a three-dimensional manger scene to honor Christ's birth. In 1223, while living in the village of Greccio, Italy, Francis of Assisi used live animals and real people to re-create the scene from that first Christmas. He also celebrated Mass at the site. It was said the setting was so true to what the manger scene in Bethlehem must have been like that

"people with their own eyes could see the privation suffered by the Holy Family." It wasn't long before neighboring churches, nobility and even retail businesses were setting up manger scenes of their own. And today, it's not uncommon for families to set aside a special place in their homes to house their own miniature version of the nativity scene.

A Classic Christmas in Greece

Because the small Turkish village of Patara was Greek territory when the man who would become Saint Nicholas was born in 280 AD, he is an extremely important Christian figure in the lives and faith of the people of Greece. While the rest of the world might revere a plump man in a red velvet suit, in Greece, Saint Nicholas is more likely portrayed wet and covered in seaweed—a fitting image for the patron saint of sailors.

Nicholas was also known for his kindness to children, earning him the additional title of patron saint of children. And despite the fact that he is honored in a more formal manner in Greece than he typically is in western churches, his feast day, December 6, is full of celebration, and "name day parties" are often held for youngsters named in his honor.

Four Wise Men?

The lesser-known story of the fourth Wise Man is perhaps one of the most relevant tales to the meaning of Christmas. The Greeks believe that four Persian astronomer-priests were studying the stars, when one particular star caught their attention, pointing the way to the birthplace of Jesus. While they were on their journey, the group passed an injured man. The three Wise Men who made it to the manger to see Jesus were the three that continued on their way, but the fourth Wise Man stopped to care for the sick man. By the time he was able to make his way to Bethlehem, the Holy Family had fled, escaping King Herod who, on hearing a "savior" was born, felt his sovereignty threatened and issued an order that all baby boys be killed.

Another version, this one from India, has the fourth Wise Man coming from a wealthy eastern family. Steeped in astrology and "sacred lore," when the fourth Wise Man saw the star, he knew it was a "sign." So he sold all his possessions and purchased three gifts for the Christ child. It was a long journey, full of obstacles and danger, but it was also full of experience. On three occasions, the fourth Wise Man came across a person in desperate need. Each time he parted with one of the gifts he had purchased for the baby Jesus. And when he finally reached the lowly stable in Bethlehem, he came to the Christ child empty handed, but with a full heart.

A Filipino version of this same legend begins in a similar vein to the Greek story, but continues on with a twist or two of its own. In this variation, the fourth Wise Man continues on and spends his entire life looking for Jesus. Throughout his life journey, he is faced with people in need, and each time this happens, he responds by reaching out to help in any way he can.

Finally, the fourth Wise Man meets with Jesus, only Jesus is not being adorned and worshipped, he is being crucified on a cross. The fourth Wise Man is devastated, knowing there is nothing he can do to help the king he so loves. Looking down, Christ smiles and tells the grieving Wise Man not to mourn. After all, he has helped Christ throughout his life. "How?" the fourth Wise Man asks. And Jesus answers:

> *For I was hungry and you gave me something to eat,*
> *I was thirsty and you gave me something to drink,*
> *I was a stranger and you invited me in,*
> *I needed clothes and you clothed me,*
> *I was sick and you looked after me,*
> *I was in prison and you came to visit me.*

– Matthew 25:35–36

Unbeknownst to the fourth Wise Man, he had been living the light of Christmas his entire life.

DID YOU KNOW?

The name of the fourth Wise Man is Artaban. Just for good measure, the names of the other three are Balthasar, Melchior and Gaspar (also Casper or Kasper).

The Sweet Sound of Children Singing

Children, in Greek culture, are considered innocent and pure. And what better way to ward off potentially evil spirits than with the voices of innocence lifted in song?

Kalanda is a derivative of the Greek word *kalo*, which means "to invite" or "to shout." In this Greek tradition, children travel door to door, treating homeowners to a festive song while at the same time bringing luck to the home. Sometimes the youngsters get a little rambunctious and sing off key—but don't worry, there's method to their madness. By performing this way, they're chasing away any *kallikantzaroi*—wicked, elf-like creatures who are known to hang about during the Christmas season.

Usually, *kalanda* occurs three times a year: on Christmas Eve, New Year's Eve and the Eve of the Epiphany, also known in Greece as Theophania.

DID YOU  KNOW?

The Greeks have other ways to ward off the *kallikantzaroi*. Just walk through any marketplace during the Christmas season, and you'll notice numerous vendors selling simple metal triangles like those we all used at one time or another in grade school music class. Legend has it that tinkling on these simple instruments will do the trick and send the *kallikantzaroi* running. Fire, light and holy water are also used to chase away the wicked creatures.

JOYEUX NOËL
in French

EASTERN EUROPE

Christmas in Slovakia

The customs of a traditional Slovak Christmas are quite intricately entwined with those of the pagan feast of winter solstice. The Christmas season begins with the feast of St. Martin's Day on November 11, which is also the beginning of the "season of the winter solstice" (November 11 is exactly 40 days before December 21, the actual winter solstice). This is followed by a succession of saint's days, culminating with a Christmas Eve celebration that quite literally lights up the day. Individual families conduct a ceremonial lighting of a fire, which may begin with lighting a fire in the family's hearth.

Another traditional lighting, of sorts, involves candles placed at the dinner table. These candles are lit during the meal. But after dinner, one of the table candles is chosen and each family member, beginning with the oldest of the household, has a chance to blow out the candle. If smoke from the extinguished candle rises, the person who blew it out will have good fortune and live to see another Christmas Eve dinner. If the smoke floats towards the floor, that person will have bad luck and not live to celebrate in the coming year. Once the fortune is told, the candle is relit and passed to the next oldest member of the family. Only after everyone has had their turn with the candle is it safe to leave the table.

A Traditional Slovak Christmas Greeting

"I greet you with the Feast of Christ's Nativity and wish that the Infant Jesus shower upon all of you His choicest blessings. May we all live in health, peace and happiness and may we all celebrate another Christmas together. A merry and blessed Christmas! Christ is born! Glorify Him!"

A Ukrainian-Style Christmas

Because tradition is so important to the people of the Ukraine, Christmas is typically celebrated according to the ancient Julian calendar. This means Ukrainian youngsters have to wait two weeks after their cousins in the West to celebrate Christ's birth and the coming New Year. Ukrainian Christmas Eve and Christmas are celebrated on January 6 and 7 respectively, with New Year's Eve and New Year's Day following a week later on January 13 and 14. Epiphany—also known in the Ukraine as the "Feast of the River Jordan"—is a celebration of Christ's baptism and is held on January 18.

Three days are typically set aside for Christmas celebrations in the traditional Ukrainian household. To prepare for the festivities, women work tirelessly to make sure every corner of the home is spotless and enough food is prepared for the family and any potential visitors. In rural areas, the men of the family tidy the yard and ensure there is enough wood cut to carry them through the three-day celebration. All this preparation is necessary so everyone is free to focus on their faith and families.

After Christmas Eve dinner, families often walk together through their neighborhoods singing *kolyadky*, which are Ukrainian Christmas carols.

While children may receive a small gift on Christmas morning, the focus of the season is the celebration of Jesus' birth. Attending Christmas mass is a highlight of Christmas Day. Families visit one another, and it's quite common for the parish priest to visit many of his parishioners and bless their households.

Out with the Old, In with the New

"As goes Christmas Eve, goes the year." This popular Polish saying highlights an important part of that country's Christmas traditions—forgiveness and reconciliation. It is believed that greeting friends and family alike, despite past differences, and moving forward in good faith will bring you goodness in the New Year. And it's hard to argue against, since it is in keeping with the Christmas spirit and makes good sense to do so.

Other traditions aren't so sensible. Polish culture is rooted in numerous superstitions, so it isn't surprising that many Christmas traditions find their origin there. For example, when grinding the poppy seed for *kutia*, an earthy pudding made of wheat, poppy seed and honey, it isn't uncommon for an unmarried daughter to be asked to complete the chore. It's believed that girls who grind poppy seed on Christmas Eve can look forward to a quick marriage.

After dinner, that same girl might step out onto her family's front porch and wait, listening for the first dog to bark. Whatever direction the bark hails from is said to be the same direction her future husband will come from.

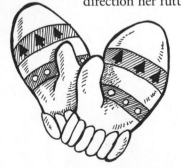

Although today, most folks in the Old Country don't really adhere to these superstitions, the traditions stemming from them have, for many, remained part of family folklore and festive fun.

Szopka

Symbolism also plays an important role in the Polish Christmas tradition. Many families take part in creating an elaborate nativity scene (or Christmas crib) called a *szopka*, which looks similar to a Russian castle whose open center is where the baby Jesus, Mary, Joseph and an entourage of other characters gather. Originating from the country's capital city of Krakow, *szopka* were first built by masons who'd found themselves temporarily unemployed because of winter weather. Using little more than odd scraps of wood, these scenes were intricately carved and crafted and then sold to the Polish elite. In an effort to keep the tradition of making *szopka* alive, an annual competition was initiated 63 years ago. Beginning on the first Thursday of December, a craftsman (or woman) might spend over 600 hours creating a *szopka* for the competition. When completed, the nativity scenes are first taken to Krakow's Market Square and then make their way to the Historical Museum, where they are judged and kept for a time on public display.

DID YOU  **KNOW?**

Scottish folk were one of the last of the Europeans to jump on board with Christmas celebrations. That's because they didn't see any reference to the celebration in the New Testament.

A Polish Feast

Oplatek are small, unleavened wafers with the figure of the Christ child, Mary and the angels or other seasonal images stamped on them. They are blessed and shared by all members of the family before the start of Christmas Eve supper, and they are also shared with the family's animals, since it is thought they were the first to welcome the Christ child.

Also known as *Wigilia*, or vigil, the Christmas Eve dinner is a sacred feast that can't begin until the first star has been spotted in the night sky. Twelve meatless dishes are served on a table often lit by candles, and a diehard traditionalist will scatter a few sprigs of hay beneath the tablecloth to symbolize Christ's birth in a manger. An extra place is also often set at the dinner table for baby Jesus, as well as for any other absent family members. That these places are set is a visual reminder of the spiritual presence of these guests.

KMB

In Poland, the Christmas season is celebrated until Epiphany, also known as Three kings Day, on January 6. Epiphany literally means "to show or reveal," and it is a celebration of the Christ child being revealed to the Wise Men. The three Wise Men, named Kaspar (or Caspar), Melchior and Balthasar, are honored by traditional Polish families, who bless their homes that day by writing the initials KMB with blessed chalk over their front doors.

I Can Tell Your Future

For practicing Christians, Christmas in Russia is steeped in an interesting mix of Christian tradition and superstition. For the Russian people, the first Sunday in Advent begins four weeks of fasting every day until sundown and mandatory daily attendance at several church services. When the first star is seen in the night sky on Christmas Eve, the fasting ends and the celebrations begin!

Strangely enough, even for those who strictly adhere to the Christian faith, fortune-telling is a big part of Russian festivities. And forget about scanning

palms or turning tarot cards. Russians have some very unique ways of telling the future. Fortune tellers in that country tell the future by dropping melted lead onto the snow or an egg yolk into a glass of water and using their individual, unique talents to decipher what the resulting squiggles and bumps mean.

DID YOU KNOW?

Talk about strange laws! As recently as 2004, folks in the city of St. Augustine, Florida, could only hang white lights outside their homes during Christmas.

Here We Go *A-Putzing*

Two items that distinguish themselves as Moravian traditions are the Moravian star and the *putz*. Thought to have originated during an evening craft class back in the 1850s, the Moravian star is a 26-pointed star made through an intricate process of folding and refolding four long, narrow strips of paper. Traditionally, each star was decorated with a lighted candle, though an electric light is used today. But instead of hanging on a tree, the Moravian star is used as the central decoration for a hallway or the porch of a home.

The word *putz* is a form of the German word *putzen* and refers to the practice of building a nativity scene. Children of the family are responsible for gathering moss, rocks, tree stumps or other items to be used as a backdrop for the nativity, but these backdrops don't have to be representative of the landscape in Bethlehem. Instead, children are encouraged to let their imaginations run wild and create to their heart's content. While they're out collecting props, the father of the family builds

a platform to hold the Holy Family and all their Christmas Eve visitors. The end result is usually prominently displayed under the Christmas tree, but it could be large enough to take up an entire room!

One Moravian pastor explained that the *putz* tells the "old, old story that transformed the world and brought to home and childhood their greatest inspiration and blessing." Since families spend part of the Christmas season going *putzing*—visiting neighbors to see their *putz*—this is a tradition that not only includes the entire family, but also entire neighborhoods and communities.

SHUB NAYA BARAS
in Hindi

AUSTRALIA

An Aussie Christmas

In many conquered lands, traditions and cultures were introduced and most often evolved into something that was unique to that country. Local, indigenous beliefs were also, at times, assimilated into the mix. Such is the case with Australian Christmas traditions.

Europeans first visited this mysterious land in the 17th century, and by 1788, had established settlements there. Among their imports were Christianity and the traditions surrounding the celebration of Christmas. Native Australians—the Aborigines and the Torres Strait Islanders—were also spiritual, but their beliefs encompassed a close relationship with nature, astronomy and the elements of earth, wind, fire and water. Today, Christmas in Australia is ultimately a very multicultural event with many traditional Christian faiths having opened themselves to include the faiths of these indigenous peoples.

THE PHILIPPINES

Simbang Gabi

Beginning on December 16, Roman Catholic churches in the Philippines hold nine separate masses, known as *Simbang Gabi,* at the crack of dawn on nine consecutive days to herald Christmas. On the last day, Christmas Eve, the Filipino people typically attend Midnight Mass, after which they celebrate long into the morning with a huge Christmas feast called *Noche Buena.*

Christmas Eve Lantern Festival

Somehow, regardless of the fact that Christmas Eve is already full of church services, food preparations and all things Christmas, the folk in San Fernando host a lantern festival. San Fernando is the capital city of the Pampanga province of the Philippines. The custom dates back to the 1800s and is directly tied to the nine masses of *Simbang Gabi*. Back then, the people of Pampanga—known as Pampangos—would parade each dawn to church, carrying brightly colored lanterns and singing hymns. Different lanterns made a showing on each day, but on Christmas Eve, the finest and most impressive would be displayed.

DID YOU KNOW?

An important tradition in the Philippines is for youngsters to visit their elderly relatives on Christmas Day. On meeting, the child will take the hand of the grandparent or godparent and raise that hand to his or her forehead. The action is a kind of blessing and is meant as a show of respect—and during Christmas, youngsters often get a special treat for doing so!

MALIGAYAMG PASKO
in Tagalog

AFRICA

Ganna, an Ethiopian Christmas

As one of the first countries outside Europe to embrace Christianity, living the faith remains very much a part of Ethiopian culture.

Ethiopia uses a calendar system based on the ancient Alexandrian calendar. Today, Ethiopia lags seven years and eight months behind the Georgian calendar adhered to by the rest of the world. Similar to the Julian calendar, the Ethiopian calendar has 12 months of 30 days each plus a 13th month that consists of five days—six days if it is a leap year. So Christmas in that country is celebrated on the 29th of Tahesas, which includes portions of what the rest of the world calls December and January. Simply put, Christmas for Ethiopians occurs on what we all know as January 7.

To commemorate the 40 days that Christ spent fasting in the desert, the 40 days leading up to Christmas (also known as *Lidet* or the "Birth of Light") are fast days. Practicing Orthodox Christians in that country are allowed only one meal a day, it cannot be consumed until after nightfall, and the meal may not include meat or dairy. At the stroke of midnight and following an extensive Christmas Eve service that lasts through the night, Ethiopians greet Christmas by feasting on a sourdough, crepe-like pancake called *injera*, which is part of the meal and is also used as a utensil of sorts to scoop up the accompanying spicy, meat stew mixture called *doro wat.*

DID YOU KNOW?

Chinese children call Santa Claus *Dun Che Lao Ren*, which literally means "Christmas old man."

Across the African Continent

With about 350 million Christians in Africa, there's no doubt that the Christmas season is a much-loved celebration. Still, practitioners of some faiths—such as the Coptic Christians in Ethiopia—celebrate on January 7, while others celebrate on December 25. And because Africa is a continent with varied faith practices, including Christianity, Islam and indigenous beliefs, Christmas is more often celebrated in the privacy of one's home rather than in a public way. Here are a few interesting African traditions:

- In Malawi, children often travel door to door, dressed in skirts made of leaves, performing traditional dances and singing traditional songs.

- In Gambia, festive folks gather for a parade, many carrying *fanals*, which are lanterns made in the shape of houses or boats.

- Folks in Kenya and Uganda often celebrate Christmas dinner with *nyama choma,* or roasted goat meat.

- In Ghana, the traditional Christmas meal includes rice, meat, fruit, porridge, okra soup or stew and a yam paste called *fufu.*

- In West Africa, it's not uncommon to see bells hanging from palm and fruit trees, or even "cotton-wool snow," bringing the North to tropical Africa.

- Woven palm fronds are the decoration of choice in Nigeria. And a Christmas meal in that country could consist of *iyan,* or pounded yam, or a delicacy known as *moin-moin*—a dish consisting of black-eyed beans mixed with vegetable oil and diced liver, prawns, chicken, fish and beef, which is then wrapped in large leaves and steamed.

Merry Christmas from Africa

The African continent is home to many countries and hundreds of languages. Here is how some Africans say "Merry Christmas":

- *Afishapa* in Akan (Ghana)

- *Merry Kisimusi* in Zimbabwe

- *Geseende Kersfees* in Afrikaans (South Africa)

- *Siniflsela Ukhisimusi Omuhle* in Zulu (South Africa)

- *Siniflsela Khisimusi Lomuhle* in Swazi (Swaziland)

- *Matswalo a Morena a Mabotse* in Sotho (Lesthoto)

- *Kuwa na Krismasi njema* in Swahili (Tanzania, Kenya)

- *Melkam Yelidet Beaal* in Amharic (Ethiopia)

- *Colo sana wintom tiebeen* in Egypt

- *E ku odun, e hu iye' dun* in Yoruba (Nigeria)

FELIZ NATAL
in Portuguese

All That
Hocus-Pocus!

*Pagan influences on Christmas are perhaps most evident
in the seemingly endless succession of superstitions
surrounding Christmas and the New Year.*

*I don't think there's a country anywhere that doesn't boast
one superstition or another. I'm just hoping my children
take it all in stride when they find that handmade spiderweb ornament attached to our Christmas tree. And I hope
they're not too disturbed when I suddenly jump up from
my chair and rush outside on a cold New Year's night and
start dancing around the tree in our front yard.*

*Perhaps I might suggest they read this section of this book
before they try to have me committed!*

CHRISTMAS MAGIC

Animal Tendencies?

Animals are apparently given some sort of extra power during the Christmas season. On Christmas Eve, cattle supposedly stop whatever they're doing, face east—towards Bethlehem—and kneel to honor the Christ child. Bees continue to hum, as bees will do, only on this special night they hum Psalm 100. Horses are believed to kneel and blow "as if to warm the manger," and animals everywhere find themselves with human voices. Anyone overhearing the animals talking to one another, however, will find themselves struck with bad luck.

A Time to be Born, a Time to Die…

While many cultures believe it's lucky to be born on Christmas Eve or Christmas Day, some find it a bad omen. The Greeks, for example, think a child born either of those days could be a *kallikantzaroi*, a kind of wandering spirit. One Polish custom warns that the child could actually be a werewolf.

Passing on at Christmas Eve might be tough on your family, but it's of considerable benefit to you if you hold to traditional Irish beliefs. Apparently, one Irish legend states that the gates of heaven open at midnight on Christmas Eve. Those who die at that time get to take a pass on purgatory and a ticket directly through the pearly gates.

DID YOU KNOW?

Because lead was at one time used in the making of tinsel, replacing the expensive silver first used in its production, the shiny decoration was banned. By the 1950s, plastic had replaced both silver and lead, and not only was tinsel available for sale once again, it was more affordable.

You Are What You Eat

Most of us can hardly wait to dig into the traditional Christmas feast we adhere to, but how much thought do we actually give to the meaning behind the food we eat? Here are a few superstitions you might want to remember before eating or not eating a particular item:

 Down a raw egg first thing on Christmas morning and you will have the strength to carry heavy weights.

 An apple eaten at midnight on Christmas Eve will keep the doctor away. Apparently, it guarantees you good health for an entire year!

 Leaving a loaf of bread on the table after Christmas Eve means an abundance of bread for the coming year.

Loving that Livestock

Talk about being cruel to be kind! Apparently sometime in distant farming history, cutting livestock and letting them bleed on Boxing Day was common practice. It was believed this would improve the animals' health and stamina! I wonder if the animals agreed with that!

Gardening Advice

It seems that burning a Yule log over Christmas has a few hidden benefits. If you collect the ashes from the log and mix them in with your seed during spring planting, you should get a bumper crop! I wonder if that applies to vegetable gardening as well?

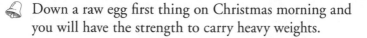

Mistletoe

He might not be Mr. Right, but if you meet him under the mistletoe, you'd better think twice before refusing a request for a kiss. One Christmas superstition states that refusing a kiss will cost a woman another month of spinsterhood! Another belief states that the single life is yours forever after such an offense. Here are a few more mistletoe warnings:

- You'd better burn your mistletoe boughs after Twelfth Night (the Eve of Epiphany) because boys or girls who kiss under them after that are sure to never marry.

- Keeping a sprig of mistletoe in a discreet corner of the house will ward away evil spirits throughout the year.

Never cut a bough of mistletoe at any time other than Christmas, or you're sure to be plagued with bad luck!

Plum Pudding

If you're planning to make plum pudding this Christmas, you'd better go about it the right way or you could find yourself with a little bad luck in the coming year.

The British have strict traditions regarding the making of plum pudding:

 The pudding should be made on the last Sunday before Advent, which was traditionally known as "Stir-up Sunday." It earned that name because of a prayer used by the Church of England on that particular day, calling the faithful to be stirred up so they may "plenteously bring forth the fruit of good works."

 Plum pudding must have 13 ingredients to represent Christ and his 12 apostles.

 Each member of the family should stir the batter—but just how you stir it is important, too! You must use a wooden spoon and stir from east to west (clockwise) to honor the three Wise Men that came from the East.

 A silver coin should be hidden inside the pudding. The lucky person to find it can expect health, wealth and happiness.

 The pudding should also have a ring, a thimble and a button hidden in it. The person who finds the ring can expect to marry in the coming year; a woman who finds the thimble will be a spinster for another year; and the unlucky guy who finds the button will have to endure another year of bachelorhood.

Proper Christmas Attire

The Greeks believe you must burn all your old shoes at Christmas to stamp out any possible bad luck in the coming year. Still another tradition states that wearing new shoes on Christmas Day will bring terrible luck. And yet another states how very important it is to line up your shoes side by side on Christmas Eve to eliminate any possibility of becoming a family that squabbles together.

Hmmm. I guess that means you burn your old shoes before bed on Christmas Day. Either that or you opt to go barefoot for a few days to satisfy all concerns surrounding shoes!

Keep the Home Fires Burning

Keeping a lighted candle on the windowsill on Christmas Eve is a rendition of a tradition that dates as far back as the origins of the winter solstice. In ancient times, the long, dark days of winter were feared, and large bonfires were used to "lure the sun back." While it's not certain when it became fairly commonplace to place a candle in the window as a beacon for weary travelers, the custom soon spread around the world. Some traditions used the candle in the window as a light for the coming Santa Claus, while others kept it there as a "symbol of welcome to Mary and Joseph as they traveled looking for shelter." For those who adhered to this tradition, it was typically the youngest member of the family who had the honor of lighting the candle, and ideally the candle was extinguished by a girl bearing the name Mary. To neglect to place a candle on your windowsill was tantamount to echoing the innkeeper from the nativity story when he told Mary and Joseph there was no room at the inn.

DID YOU KNOW?

Christmas, like Hanukkah, is also referred to as the "Festival of Light" by Christians. The use of light in the form of candles and lamps, and later electrical bulbs, was thought to represent the Star of Bethlehem and, subsequently, the light of Christ.

Strolling Trolls

Strange to think that evil may lurk in the most pastoral of settings, but an old Swedish superstition warns against wandering into the countryside to catch a Christmas morning sunrise. That's because in Sweden, wicked elves or trolls are believed to wander about between cock crow and daybreak on that day.

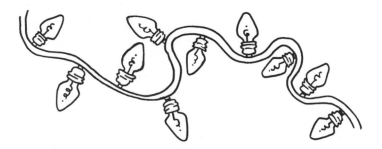

Itsy, Bitsy Spider

According to Ukrainian folklore, despite all the cleaning preparations that must take place before Christmas, it's actually good luck to find a spiderweb thriving in a corner somewhere in the house. The story behind this superstition revolves around a poor woman who couldn't afford to provide decorations for her family's Christmas tree. On Christmas morning, she woke to find that as the first light of the sun struck the cobwebs, they turned to silver. A spider and his web had decorated the tree overnight, bringing the family good luck.

Today, it's not uncommon for traditional Ukrainian families to decorate their Christmas trees with spiderwebs made of silver glitter and fine wire no thicker than a human hair. The decoration guarantees a spiderweb in the house—and the good luck that comes with it!

DID YOU KNOW?

In some countries, Christmas Eve is considered a night of magic when even animals are able to speak!

Pie, Anyone?

The delectable dessert known as mince pie comes with a tradition—and a superstition—of its own.

Initially, mince pies were known as "Christmas pye" and were more of a dinner dish than a dessert. This dish originated in England back in the medieval period and was originally made with ox tongue, chicken, liver or other chopped meat, an assortment of fruit and various spices. Because of their exotic spiciness, the resulting creations were thought of as "edible symbols of the Wise Men." In honor of the pie's origin, some more traditional bakers still use lean ground beef in the fruity, spiced pastry of today—and believe me, you'd never know there was meat in that tart!

Legend has it that an individual who managed to eat a mince pie on each of the 12 days of Christmas would be blessed with 12 happy months. Hopefully, that didn't refer to the original full-sized pie, but the much smaller tart of more recent years!

Oh, and one more thing. Just like its cousin the plum pudding, you absolutely *must* stir the ingredients in a clockwise direction or you are asking for trouble in the following year!

DID YOU KNOW?

The 1901 five-minute silent film entitled *A Holiday Pageant at Home* is thought to be the first Christmas movie.

Decorating Dos and Don'ts

Traditionally, erecting and decorating your family Christmas tree before December 24 and letting it remain in your home after January 6—also known as Twelfth Night or the Eve of Epiphany—was considered bad luck.

Of course, most folks in the western world don't adhere to that belief. In fact, some families in the United States put up their trees sometime during the fourth week of November, just after Thanksgiving. In Canada and in many European homes, it's not uncommon for families to decorate for the holidays in early to mid-December and leave their decorations up until early January.

It appears the folks in Germany hang on to their seasonal decorations the longest. A tradition from the sixth century called "Candlemas" holds that the Christmas season doesn't officially end until February 2, after Mary completed a 40-day purification rite. Families adhering to that tradition don't take their trees down until then!

Something to Crow About!

Russian families not wanting to "get caught with egg on their faces" had a unique way of determining what the coming year held for them. The young ladies of the family would gather some of the family's grain and make five equal piles on the kitchen floor, carrying out a tradition appropriately called "five piles of grain." Each pile represented a hope for the New Year: wealth, poverty, death, marriage or another year of being single.

At midnight, a family member would make a trip to the henhouse, collect a hen and return to the house. At this point, the poor, sleeping hen was ready to "get its hackles up" and "fly the coop, " being more than a little miffed and considerably confused at having been so rudely removed from its comfortable nest. Still, it wasn't about to get a reprieve—not yet! The anxious Russian family would let the hen loose and wait anxiously for it to settle on one of the five piles of grain and thereby tell the family's future.

Not wanting to "count their chickens before they're hatched," no one in the family would predict where the hen would choose to "rule the roost." Either way, the poor chicken had something to cackle about when the family removed her, yet again, and booted her back into the barn.

And that's no "cock and bull" story!

Going on the Wren

A particularly odd Irish tradition that dates back hundreds of years is associated with Saint Stephen's Day (December 26). It centers around bands of young boys with blackened faces, dressed in tattered and worn women's clothing, marching from house to house with a dead wren dangling on a string tied to a pole. Once they attracted the attention of the lady of the house, they sang:

> *The wren, the wren, the king of all birds,*
> *Saint Stephen's Day was caught in the furze,*
> *Although he is little, his family is great,*
> *I pray you, good landlady, give us a treat.*

The expectation was that they'd receive food, a drink (and believe it or not, in decades past this was sometimes an alcoholic drink) and money. If these gifts weren't immediately forthcoming, the Wren Boys, as they were commonly referred to, would continue with a second verse of their ancient rhyme. Yet another verse was reserved for those times when they may have received a treat but it wasn't considered sufficient.

Here's where the tradition gets even more unique, if that's at all possible. A household that treated the Wren Boys well would receive a feather from the dead bird. Now before you turn up your nose at the thought, it was believed this would bring good luck to the household. Refuse to take part in the tradition and look out! You could find yourself facing serious retribution if the Wren Boys decide to bury the dead bird in your yard. As you can imagine, this was most definitely bad luck!

DID YOU KNOW?

You've likely heard of Father Christmas and understand it is another name for Santa Claus. But where did this version of the seasonal fellow come from? Father Christmas is an amalgamation of pagan gods—the giant Saturnalia, who appeared once a year and was known to enjoy his food and drink, and Odin, a rather ambivalent god who was said to wander about during the winter months. It's Father Christmas that youngsters in the United Kingdom, Australia, New Zealand and assorted other Commonwealth countries wait for on Christmas Eve.

Wren Dances

It wasn't uncommon for the Wren Boys to continue their rounds into the night, covering several miles. As you can imagine, they'd be a tired lot, so the custom of having a Wren Dance on the day after Saint Stephen's night (December 26) gave them a chance to freshen up a little before they partied. At times, the groups of boys would pool whatever money they collected in order to pay for the dance, and the entire community was usually invited.

DID YOU  KNOW?

While China is not a traditionally Christian country, many Chinese do celebrate Christmas, and a significant part of that celebration is focused on symbolically bringing the "light of Christ" into the home. The Chinese call their Christmas tree a "Tree of Light," and paper lanterns are often used as decorations.

Why Kill a Wren?

There are a number of explanations for how the tradition of killing a wren came about.

In one scenario, Irish soldiers were attempting to sneak up on sleeping Viking invaders. It was a wren that was said to have put the kibosh on that idea, waking one Viking soldier by pecking at breadcrumbs that had somehow collected on his helmet.

Another legend tells of how the wren revealed the whereabouts of Saint Stephen, who was taking cover behind a bush to hide from his enemies.

And, of course, there's at least one tie to pre-Christian customs. According to this legend, it was pagan tradition to sacrifice something sacred at the end of the year. In Irish folklore, the wren is called the "king of birds"—but it is only fair to point out it received that honor in a rather sneaky way. According to the legend, a contest was held among all the birds to decide which one should be named king. The bird that could fly the highest would earn this honor. By now you're likely wondering how the wren managed that feat. Well, you've got to give him credit for ingenuity. Knowing he couldn't beat the mighty eagle, he just tucked himself away under the eagle's wing and waited for the right moment to make an appearance. When the eagle had flown as high as he could go, the wren flew out from under the eagle's wing and soared even higher, earning the coveted title. Ironically enough, being "king of birds" also meant a considerable number of these "sacred creatures" would be sacrificed each year as the Wren Boys made their rounds. Ain't life interesting?

Gift Giving

The phrase "It's the thought that counts" definitely describes the first gift giving at Christmastime. The tradition, which extends back to the Roman winter festivals of Saturnalia (in December) and Kalends (in January), began with something as simple as twigs from the trees in a sacred grove, which were exchanged as good luck wishes between friends. The type of gifts given at this time of the year increased in size and stature throughout the years. But when Christians first began giving gifts over the Christmas season, the practice was initially frowned upon because of its connection to this earlier pagan tradition. Still, some argued that the Magi brought gifts to Jesus—surely this was Christian justification for the practice. And by the Middle Ages, gift giving during the season had gained a general acceptance.

DID YOU KNOW?

Horses in Europe are sometimes treated to a drink of beer on Christmas.

Hogueras

Hogueras, otherwise known as bonfires, are a common sight in Spain during the winter solstice. The Spanish believe that men and women alike should leap over these bonfires to protect themselves against illness in the coming year.

Srozhdestvom vym
in Ukrainian

ADVICE FOR THE NEW YEAR

Bills, Bills, Bills and Other Distresses

Whatever you do, don't write a check for the gas bill—or any other bill for that matter—on January 1. All bills should be up to date before the stroke of midnight. If not, and you pay a debt on New Year's Day, money will flow out of the house all year long!

Then there's the warning against breaking something on New Year's Day or crying on the first day of the year. The superstition is that you'll go on breaking things and crying all year long.

I think there are enough warnings in this vein that it's safe to say if you don't want to see something repeat itself throughout the year, you'd best be sure it doesn't happen on day one!

What's in Your Cupboard?

No matter what it takes, you must make sure your cupboards, fridge and freezer are well stocked on New Year's Day. Oh, and check everyone's wallets to make sure they contain plenty of money. This custom is said to ensure the coming year will be a prosperous one.

DID YOU  KNOW?

Contrary to some New Year's superstitions, the Irish believe that every bit of food in their home must be eaten on *Oliche na Coda Moire* or "Night of the Bid Portion," which is New Year's Eve. For the Irish, an empty cupboard on January 1 means months of plenty ahead.

Fan Those Flames

If you want to keep those flames of love a-burnin' between you and your spouse or significant other, you'd better be ready to smooch it up as soon as the clock strikes midnight on New Year's Eve. Legend has it that if you don't, the coming year could get rather chilly.

Death and Dying

Morbidness seems to be the order of the day when it comes to some New Year's superstitions. For example, doing the laundry is particularly bad luck since, as the saying goes, a member of the family could get "washed away," as it were, in the coming months.

Other deadly beliefs:

- If the main candle in the household goes out during the Christmas season, it could mean the death of the head of that household.

- If you're seated around a fire and someone casts a headless shadow—well, you can guess what that predicts!

Bring on Those Black-Eyed Peas

And no, I don't mean the hip-hop group. According to one American superstition, eating a helping of black-eyed peas on New Year's Day will bring good luck and money, too!

Every Way the Wind Blows

If you just imagine for a moment everyone doing this, our neighborhoods would appear very strange indeed. But according to one superstition, you should sneak outside very early on the morning of New Year's Day and check which way the wind is blowing.

- 🔔 A north wind means a year of bad weather;

- 🔔 A south wind means good weather and prosperity;

- 🔔 An east wind means famine and bad luck;

- 🔔 A west wind means there'll be no shortage of milk and fish, but an important person will die;

- 🔔 No wind means joy and prosperity for everyone.

Don't Mind the Neighbors

New Year's Eve is one time when you want noise to be the order of the night. One superstition states that everyone should make as much noise as possible to ward off evil spirits.

Tree Dancing

No, your neighbor hasn't lost her marbles—or had too much to drink during her New Year's Day festivities. She's just dancing around the tree in her front yard to ensure that she's lucky in love, healthy as a horse and prosperous in the year ahead.

DID YOU KNOW?

The Christmas tradition of lighting candles was adopted from pagan custom. In pagan tradition, candles were lit to drive away the forces of cold and darkness. Christians later adopted the practice, but for them the candle symbolized Jesus as the "Light of the World."

Spic and Span

By all means, sweep those floors and tidy up the house for company. Just make sure you're done your household chores early on December 31. That way, you remove the danger of sweeping good luck from the house.

World of Work

Take a second to ponder your life at the workplace, read a pertinent article or write yourself a reminder note—just do some small thing that's work-related on New Year's Day and pave the way for a successful year. But don't get too carried away, since starting a serious project that day is bad luck.

Kala Christouyenna
in Greek

Music, Movies and Beloved Tales

Who says reality TV is a new thing? Really, when you think about it, every movie, story, legend and even folksong is grounded in reality. What is a story if it isn't the unveiling of a person's life or a situational dilemma, even if that person or situation is fictional? And with a subject as suggestive as Christmas, it's no wonder there are so many touching tales told through story and song.

What makes a tale even more interesting is when the story behind its inception touches the heart as well. What you'll find in this section is exactly that—the stories behind the stories. Why does the tale of Rudolph the Red-Nosed Reindeer touch us so personally? Why are we offended when we're called a Scrooge? And how did the beloved carol "Silent Night" come to be a favorite hymn worldwide?

So put on the kettle and get ready for some heartwarming tales behind the tales we all know and love.

MUSIC

Come Let Us Adore Him!

Despite the fact that the Christmas carol "O Come All Ye Faithful" is also known by the Latin name "Adeste, Fideles," the seasonal favorite doesn't actually hail from anywhere near Rome, or any other part of Italy for that matter. However, this knowledge is a fairly recent acquisition.

For many years it was thought the carol was written by a 13th-century Italian scholar named Bonaventura. Of course, not everyone agreed with that theory and others were developed. Some thought the Cistercian order of monks, who lived in France, were responsible. For a time the hymn was even nick-named "The Portuguese Hymn" by the English, crediting a Portuguese birth for this creation. Ironically enough, it was actually an Englishman named John Francis Wade who eventually got credit for this masterpiece of seasonal song.

A Catholic layman facing persecution in England, John Francis Wade moved to France and made a living by copying and selling sheet music. It is believed he wrote his famous hymn between 1740 and 1743. With his connections to numerous Catholic musicians, he could likely have had a number of people write music to the piece, but some historians believe John Francis Wade wrote both the words and music.

By the time he died in 1786, at the age of 75, Wade had moved from France back to his Lancashire home and was well known throughout the country for his contribution to annual Christmas festivities. Today, there are more than 50 translations of the beloved hymn. And every Christmas, in churches around the world, the faithful sing:

O come let us adore Him, Christ the Lord.

Stille Nacht, Heilig Nacht
(Silent Night, Holy Night)

True brilliance often comes with a single spark—a chance circumstance, a brief opportunity, an idea that blossoms into a life of its own—and though credit is assigned to the person or persons who brought that idea to the public, often they themselves point to a greater power as having blessed them with the initial inspiration. Such was the case of a teacher named Franz Gruber and a priest named Joseph Mohr.

The story goes that in Oberndorf, Austria, on the cold Christmas Eve of 1818, the only organ available to parishioners at Saint Nicholas Church had been damaged by the flooding of the nearby Salzach River. But this was Christmas! "How would the faithful celebrate the holiest day of the church year without music?" Father Mohr wondered.

So concerned was he, that he took off on foot, traveling the two miles from his home in Oberndorf to Arnsdorf, where his organist, Franz Gruber, was usually busy with his students. A very nervous Father Mohr presented the talented musician with the words to a hymn he himself had written and asked Gruber if he could put the words to music. Father Mohr was taking a chance, to be sure. Having written the hymn two years earlier, he had yet to share his lyrics with anyone, much less a packed church on Christmas Eve. Would his humble efforts be a pleasing offering to the Christ child?

It took Gruber just a few hours to compose a guitar melody for the words, and he even had time to practice the new hymn with the choir before the service. And on December 24, 1818, "Silent Night"—the hymn that is sung in every Christian church at least once during the Christmas season—was born.

Legend has it that a master organ builder who'd visited the church repeatedly trying to repair the organ heard the hymn and made a copy for himself. It was then adopted by a family of traveling musicians and, with a few minor changes, evolved into the melody we know today. By the turn of the century, the hymn was said to have been spread by Christian missionaries throughout the Americas and to England, Africa and even New Zealand.

Father Mohr never received recognition during his lifetime for writing the lyrics, having died before the hymn became widely popular. Mozart, Haydn and even Beethoven were suspected to have composed the music, and it wasn't until 1994, when an original arrangement in Gruber's own handwriting was authenticated, that Gruber was formally recognized as the composer.

One Very Good King

At first glance, other than a reference to the Feast of Stephen, which takes place on the day after Christmas (so some may argue this is actually a Boxing Day hymn), it's not immediately obvious why "Good King Wenceslas" is such a beloved Christmas carol. There's no reference to the birth of Christ, nor any direct reference to his teachings. But a good reading of the verses, and a little knowledge of the history behind the words, is enough to develop a true appreciation for the carol in almost anyone's heart.

Let's begin with the history.

King Wenceslas was the Duke of Bohemia from 922 to 935 AD, though some scholars believe he died earlier, in 929 AD. Either way, he was known as a good and noble king who ruled fairly and was concerned about the welfare of all his subjects. The carol tells the story of how the king went far beyond what most, even then, would see as the responsibility of nobility.

The incident took place "on the Feast of Stephen," when King Wenceslas literally peered out his window and saw a poor man gathering wood for a fire. Believing that Christian faith must be teamed with action and accompanied only by his page (who on the journey was warmed by the footsteps of his master), the king braved the darkness of night and the perils of a winter storm to bring the pauper a feast to enjoy and logs for a warm fire.

It wasn't until many, many years after King Wenceslas was killed by his own evil brother that his story was immortalized by John M. Neale in 1853. The words were then set to the tune of a 13th-century "spring carol" entitled "Spring Has Unwrapped Her Flowers."

And so, though there's no mention of Christ in this carol, His teachings are exemplified in the actions of a noble king who most clearly understood that it is more blessed to give than to receive:

Therefore, Christian men, be sure, wealth or rank possessing,
Ye who now will bless the poor, shall yourself find blessing.

DID YOU  KNOW?

In Australia, lifeguards often give Santa's reindeer the night off and row him ashore so he can make it to every youngster's home on Christmas Eve. But in Australia, anything can happen. And when it comes to making a grand entry, Santa has been known to skydive his way into this land Down Under.

'Twas in the Moon of Wintertime

The history of the European settlement of Canada is, sadly, tarnished by misunderstanding and often the mistreatment of First Nations peoples. In an effort to re-create the standard of living they'd had in their homeland, early settlers often overlooked the strife they caused to a way of life that, though foreign to them, was valued and treasured by the aboriginal population of Canada. The imported Christian church and the teachings of Jesuit missionaries could be said to be guilty of the same sins. On the other hand, not all newcomers to the country were blind to the beauty of culture and depth of spirit exhibited by Canada's original inhabitants. A Jesuit missionary named Jean de Brebeuf was one of those insightful souls.

Living among the Huron people in the mid 17th century, Jean de Brebeuf drew on Huron culture in creating Canada's first, original Christmas carol. Known as "The Huron Carol," the lyrics tie in the "mighty Gitchi Manitou"—the Great Spirit of the Huron people—in a retelling of the Christmas story. In this version, baby Jesus is wrapped in "a ragged robe of rabbit skin" and "chiefs from far before Him knelt," replacing the Wise Men of the Bible. The words demonstrated a great respect for the indigenous peoples, who were as much children of God as their cousins from across the Atlantic Ocean.

The Huron readily accepted the hymn, and it became a part of their oral tradition. It wasn't translated and written down until many years later, long after Jean de Brebeuf was killed in a conflict between the Huron and the Iroquois in 1649.

Today, the hymn is a treasured part of First Nations culture, and the rest of Canada is more than happy to share in that tradition.

One Horse Open Sleigh

When the familiar favorite carol "Jingle Bells" was written in 1857, it was known by the title "One Horse Open Sleigh." The song's American author, James Pierpont, intended it to be sung at his Boston church during Thanksgiving, but everyone loved it, especially the children, and it was decided the song would be sung at the upcoming Christmas service. It wasn't long before its popularity grew beyond the small church community.

While James Pierpont wrote the lyrics, Oliver Ditson composed and published the music for "One Horse Open Sleigh." But this original composition was a far more classical version than the tune we know today. By the second printing of the sheet music, the title had already been changed to "Jingle Bells"—the popular name it had been given by the public. Still, it's not clear when the tune evolved into its current version or who was responsible.

Whichever name you prefer, this Yuletide favorite has secured a special place in the Smithsonian National Air and Space Museum in downtown Washington, DC. Its claim to fame is being the first song of any genre to be performed and broadcast from outer space. Prior to their big gig on December 16, 1965, Tom Stafford and Wally Schirra, two astronauts on *Gemini 6*, contacted Mission Control with this report: "We have an object, looks like a satellite going from north to south; probably in polar orbit… I see a command module and eight smaller modules in front. The pilot of the command module is wearing a red suit…"

Using only a miniature harmonica just over an inch long and a strand of six jingle bells, the pair performed their one-of-a kind concert. Both instruments, along with a number of additional items from that mission, have been donated to the Smithsonian and are on display there.

Twelve Days of Christmas

Religious persecution is a sad reality for many faiths around the world, and the Christian church has been both the persecutor and the persecuted. To remain faithful to their beliefs, yet to escape persecution and even possible death, followers of some faiths have resorted to using code words to represent something altogether different. One legend suggests that the fun and quirky song "The Twelve Days of Christmas" is a prime example of just such a practice, beginning with the name itself, which represents the 12 days between the birth of Christ and Epiphany, the arrival of the Wise Men. The rest of the song was believed to be a kind of "secret catechism," representing key beliefs of the Catholic Church. Here is what the folklore suggests:

🔔 The partridge represents Jesus Christ;

🔔 The two turtledoves represent the Old and New Testaments;

The three French hens represent the virtues of faith, hope and charity;

The four Gospels and their evangelist authors are the four calling birds;

The Pentateuch, the first five books of the Old Testament, is represented by the five golden rings;

The six geese a-laying are the six days of creation;

The seven sacraments and the seven gifts of the Holy Spirit are represented by the swimming swans;

The eight milking maids represent the eight beatitudes;

The nine ladies dancing represent the nine fruits of the Holy Spirit;

The 10 commandments are represented by the leaping lords;

The 11 faithful disciples are represented by the piping pipers;

The 12 drummers drumming point to the 12 statements of belief in the Apostle's Creed.

There are many academic arguments refuting this claim. One scholar questioned how "maids a-milking," for example, could remind anyone of the eight beatitudes. It's been further argued that if a society banned all things Christian, would not the celebration of Christmas—and any and all songs relating to that celebration—be banned as well?

Regardless of the academic and theological arguments surrounding this particular story, many Christians still believe the legend holds true. And when you really think about the suggested meanings behind the simple rhyme, regardless their origin, it appears they only enhance the "reason for the season."

The "Twelve Days of Christmas" Down Under

Aussies have added their own unique twist to the traditional "Twelve Days of Christmas" carol. So if you're looking for an international twist to your custom of caroling, how about adding this last verse:

On the twelfth day of Christmas, my true love sent to me:
Twelve koalas clowning,
Eleven lizards leaping,
Ten dingoes dancing,
Nine numbats knitting,
Eight quokkas cooking,
Seven mice a-marching,
Six penguins peeping,
Five crocodiles,
Four pelicans,
Three lorikeets,
Two wallabies,
And a bellbird in a flame tree.

For the majority of us who might not know what a quokka, numbat or any of the other unique references here are, make sure you have a good dictionary handy—or a computer hooked up to the Internet. You might want to finish off the night doing a little research while sipping on your hot toddy!

White Christmas

The beloved Christmas carol "White Christmas" was originally composed by the great musician and lyricist Irving Berlin in 1942 for the movie *Holiday Inn*—the story of an inn that only opens during the holiday season. Bing Crosby starred in the film, and though it fared well—as evidenced by the fact that an entire franchise adopted the name for their chain of hotels—it was the sentiment behind the carol "White Christmas" that struck a chord with the soldiers fighting in World War II and the families who were waiting for them back home. The song's popularity was seemingly endless, and in 1954, it was used again, this time in the movie bearing its name, *White Christmas*.

For more than 50 years, the song "White Christmas," featuring Crosby's deep, rich voice accompanied by the John Scott Trotter Orchestra and the Ken Darby Singers, was the best-selling single in any music category.

Today the movie, along with the song, has earned a place in the annals of Christmas classics of the modern age.

DID YOU KNOW?

Boxing Day may mean just that in Australia—a day for boxing. On the other hand, football (soccer), biking or a good game of cricket sounds good as well. In that country, the annual Boxing Day holiday means a day off from work to enjoy all things sporting! What a way to work off Christmas dinner!

The Favorite Reindeer

Christmas might be a time when most of us spend a little more than our budget allows, but in 1939, management at the Chicago-based Montgomery Ward company didn't want to loosen their purse strings any more than absolutely necessary. So instead of buying Christmas coloring books from a distributor to give out to their customers, they decided to draw on talent a little closer to home and produce the books on their own. Enter Robert L. May.

The story goes that the 24-year-old advertising copywriter drew on his own experiences as a boy of small stature who was often teased. The children's story *The Ugly Duckling* was another influence. And so May went to work, bouncing ideas and rhymes off his four-year-old daughter Barbara, and the children's Christmas favorite "Rudolph the Red-Nosed Reindeer" was born.

Unfortunately, because Robert May was an employee of Montgomery Ward, the copyright of the story belonged to them. May's wife became ill and died just around the time he created his famous story, and the money from a copyright would have brought May and his daughter a little financial security. It wasn't until 1947 that May finally talked the company's president, Sewell Avery, into turning the copyright over to him. By then, six million copies of the story had already been circulated.

The story was first printed on a commercial scale in 1947, and a nine-minute cartoon shown in theatres before the feature attraction was produced in 1948. The song bearing the same name was written around that time by May's brother-in-law, Johnny Marks, securing the story and the beloved character in the hearts of children everywhere and for all time.

DID YOU KNOW?

Apparently, back in the 18th century, folks in Germany didn't think the tree trimming was complete until there were at least 400 candles secured to the branches of a 12-foot-high tree.

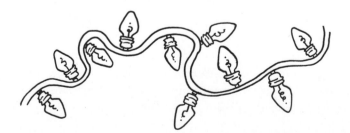

Auld Lang Syne

While the words of the traditional Scottish rendition of this beloved New Year's ballad might leave many of us scratching our heads in wonder, hearing the song typically sung at the stroke of midnight is enough to bring tears to most eyes.

The title "Auld Lang Syne" can be translated a number of ways: "old long since," "old long ago," "times gone by" or "days gone by." Though the song is typically attributed to Scotland's most famous poet, Robert Burns, he actually only contributed two of the song's five verses.

Robert (or Robbie) Burns lived from 1759 to 1796 and was both prolific and beloved during his short life. He was also honest, and though he was often credited with penning the song, he never laid claim to its authorship. In a letter to the Scots Musical Museum, he explained its origins as follows: "The following song, an old song, of the olden times, and which has never been in print, nor even in manuscript until I took it down from an old man's singing, is enough to recommend any air."

Still, Robert Burns was responsible for bringing the song to popularity in Scotland. But it was a Canadian, Guy Lombardo, and his band the Royal Canadians, who first played the tune at a New Year's Eve gala at the Hotel Roosevelt Grill in New York City on December 31, 1929, and unwittingly propelled the song to the popularity it enjoys today.

While it fits so naturally with the theme of New Year's Eve and is sung in Scotland during Hogmanay, "Auld Lang Syne" has been adopted as an anthem of sorts by a number of groups.

The Indian Armed Forces plays the piece during their Passing-out Parade—a parade traditionally held in front of commanding officers following a course of training. "Auld Lang Syne" is even used as the University of Virginia fight song.

DID YOU  KNOW?

Santa has been known to arrive in Hawaii and Australia on a surfboard.

GOD JUL
in Swedish

WELL-LOVED STORIES

Merry Christmas, Everyone!

You're a Scrooge. Don't be a Scrooge. Bah, humbug! These and other similar phrases have evolved into everyday language to such an extent that even if you've never heard of Charles Dickens and his beloved story *A Christmas Carol* and don't participate in the festive season, chances are you still know what they mean.

It took Charles Dickens six weeks of concentrated effort to pen his Christmas classic and, depending on the source, anywhere from the first 24 hours to the first week after the 162-page novel hit the store shelves on December 17, 1843, for all 6000 copies in that initial printing to sell out. The intricate tale of a miserly old man being visited by three ghosts on Christmas Eve and the lives of his clerk, Bob Cratchit, and the Cratchit family, tugged at the heartstrings of readers, critics and other authors of the day. The story had the capacity to cast such a spell that Dickens himself is reported to have said he "wept and laughed and wept again," and that the evolving manuscript thrilled him in a "most extraordinary manner."

Today, the story continues to captivate audiences across the world. Since 1910, several dozen film adaptations have hit television and movie screens. The 1951 British version of the classic, featuring Alastair Sim as Scrooge, is still considered by many to be the best adaptation of the story.

Dickens went on to write four other Christmas novels—*The Chimes* in 1844, *The Cricket on the Hearth* in 1845, *The Battle of Life* in 1846 and *The Haunted Man* in 1848. As well, he penned another 21 Christmas-themed short stories between 1848 and 1867. But despite the vast number of creations birthed throughout his prolific career, *A Christmas Carol* ranks as one of his best-known works and certainly his most well-known Christmas story.

In case you're interested, and if you ever find yourself in the neighborhood of Madison Avenue and 36th Street in New York City, check out the Morgan Library. Dickens' original, autographed manuscript is reportedly housed there.

And regardless of your affinity for literature, or your love of the Christmas season, if we all had the opportunity to see our faults and overcome them—to learn how to "keep Christmas well," as it were—perhaps the concept of peace on earth would become reality.

Yes, Virginia

Perhaps the most beloved Christmas story of modern times is the true story of eight-year-old Virginia O'Hanlon and her quest to confirm the existence of Santa Claus. Snow had yet to dust the ground in the early fall of 1897 in New York City when Virginia confronted her father with a most serious question: Did Santa Claus really exist? Some of her friends had lost their faith in the jolly spirit, and knowing of their disappointment, Virginia's own beliefs had begun to waver.

Her father suggested she write a letter to the editor of their daily newspaper, *The Sun*. "If you see it in *The Sun*, it's so," he assured. So Virginia took his advice and wrote a letter, and the reply appeared in the paper's editorial pages that year and every year thereafter until the newspaper closed up shop in 1949. Although it wasn't known until after his death in 1906, the full-length editorial reply was penned by Francis Pharcellus Church. "Yes, Virginia, there is a Santa Claus," Church convincingly argued. "He exists as certainly as love and generosity and devotion exist…"

DID YOU KNOW?

When Santa visits Australia, he sometimes gives his reindeer a break and employs eight kangaroos to pull his sleigh.

Miracle on 34th Street

While Virginia O'Hanlon was questioning the existence of Santa Claus, Susan Walker—the eight-year-old character of the film *Miracle on 34th Street*—was outright adamant he was nothing more than the fiction of legend and folklore. In the movie, Kris Kringle, Macy's parade-riding store Santa, on the other hand, is just as adamant that Santa Claus lives because, after all, he is Santa Claus.

Miracle on 34th Street was written by American author Valentine Davies. The movie pairs Natalie Wood as Susan Walker and 72-year-old Edmund Gwen as Kris Kringle in a journey of sorts through the wonder of Christmas, where dreams really do come true and happily ever after is quite possible—almost as possible as the existence of Santa Claus.

The original movie aired in 1947, and though there have been many remakes, the original version remains the hands-down favorite.

What Would It Be Like Had I Never Been Born?
In a desperate moment, when life's struggles seem almost too much to bear, many of us may have pondered this very question. This question forms the premise of the 1946 movie *It's a Wonderful Life,* directed by Frank Capra. The film, an adaptation of a 1938 short story entitled "The Greatest Gift," by Philip Van Doren Stern, finds Jimmy Stewart cast in the main role of George Bailey. A distraught Bailey, frustrated by the monotony and boredom of his life, meets an angel after attempting to throw himself off a bridge. Through that fortuitous encounter, Bailey gets the opportunity to see the lives of his family and friends as they would be had he never existed. Of course, the end result is an epiphany for Bailey, who comes to see his life as one of value after all, and he is given a chance at redemption when he is allowed to return to it. Sound familiar? It should.

The storyline has been compared to an American version of Charles Dickens' *A Christmas Carol*.

But Capra wasn't the first to bring Stern's 24-page short story to the big screen. For years, Stern had tried to get his creation into print, and when in 1943, Stern still couldn't find a publisher, he printed 200 copies himself and sent them off as Christmas gifts to his friends and family. Those who received copies thought it was a brilliant story, including his agent Shirley Collier. It was through her insistence that Stern agreed to sell the story to a Hollywood studio.

The film first appeared as *The Greatest Gift* in 1944, and the short story was also published that year in *Good Housekeeping* magazine under the title "The Man Who Never Was." Capra didn't get a shot at obtaining the screen rights until 1945, when he returned from a tour of duty in World War II. Capra's first goal was to expand the storyline, which he did with help from screenwriters Albert Hackett and Frances Goodrich. The end result was the Christmas tale that reminds all viewers who know and love it that what's most important in life is our friends and family.

DID YOU KNOW?

If you actually got every gift named in *The Twelve Days of Christmas*, you would bag 364 gifts.

Interviewing Santa

What if you could ask Santa anything you wanted? How old is he? Where do all his elves sleep? How does he make it around the entire world in just one magical night? It was this premise—the chance to ask Santa every question that could ever come to mind—that formed the foundation for the Christmas classic *An Interview with Santa Claus*, by Margaret Mead and Rhoda Metraux. The two women were contributing editors for *Redbook* magazine, and they wrote the story for the December 1977 edition in a question-answer format, with Mead and Metraux serving as the interviewers and Santa Claus as the interviewee. The book explains everything from the origins of Santa to the practicality of using reindeer as his main mode of travel and is written as if the authors were speaking to three-year-old Kate—Metraux's granddaughter and Mead's goddaughter. The story was published the following year in book form in both Canada and the U.S.

You'll Shoot Your Eye Out!

All I want for Christmas is…. In the case of Ralphie Parker, the main character of the 1983 Christmas classic *A Christmas Story*, the perfect gift for this wide-eyed nine-year-old dreamer is a Red Ryder Carbine Action 200-Shot, Range Model Air Rifle. Written by Jean Shepherd, the story explores what some may see as the increasing commercialization of Christmas, while at the same time capturing a child's imagination during the season. The story has fast become a favorite festive tale for today's generation—just ask any number of Hollywood celebrities.

In fact, it's become such a modern, cultural classic that the Cleveland, Ohio, house where the movie was filmed has been purchased and is being restored to the way it was in the movie—exactly. In fact, those involved have even suggested that anyone interested in contributing an item or two watch reruns of the movie to ensure they donate just the right stuff! You can also log on to www.achristmasstoryhouse.com and take a virtual tour of the movie-set-turned-museum. Jean Shepherd, who died in 1999, would no doubt be proud!

DID YOU  KNOW?

The fact that everyone wants to lay claim to Santa sometimes leaves him in a bit of a quandary. So to keep everyone happy, he has a few headquarters, one of which is located in the town of Rovaniemi, Lapland, Finland. At that location alone, more than 700,000 letters from Santa-lovers in 200 countries are received!

The Grinch

"You're a mean one, Mr. Grinch"—and thanks to Dr. Seuss, the world is well aware of that fact, along with your complete redemption! First published in 1957, *How the Grinch Stole Christmas* is one of those bedtime tales youngsters love to fear. It's absolutely incomprehensible, in the mind of a wide-eyed child who is having trouble maintaining some level of patience while counting down the days to the big event, to imagine a creature who hates Christmas. And if such a creature did indeed exist, he must be just as Dr. Seuss describes him—with a heart "two sizes too small."

Of course, we all know that despite the Grinch's malevolent plan to scoop up all the decorations, gifts and food in Whoville in an effort to stop Christmas from coming, in the end, he learns that Christmas is about much more than the festive wrapping—it's about life and love and peace on earth, goodwill to all. And for all the finely tailored storytelling genius of its author, *How the Grinch Stole Christmas* is more than just a tall tale—it's a wonderful example of the Christmas message. Metro-Goldwyn-Mayer's MGM Animation/Visual Arts studio certainly thought so. In 1966, they adapted the story for an animated television special starring Boris Karloff as the narrator. It was first released on December 23, 1966. Since then, the

story has been adapted into numerous formats and translated into several languages. But for many—especially those of us who grew up in the 1960s and remember that first airing—the MGM adaptation remains a seasonal favorite.

DID YOU KNOW?

Theodor Geisel was the author *How the Grinch Stole Christmas*. Of course, he decided to adopt his mother's maiden name of Seuss and is better known by his pen name Dr. Seuss.

CHUNG MUNG GIANG SINH
in Vietnamese

Looking Back
on Christmases
of Yesterday

While tradition and family folklore give us a peek into the past and an understanding of how much things change over the years, try perusing your local antique market and checking out an old magazine or two. You'll get a laugh, that's for sure.

The following reflections come from past issues of the British Good Housekeeping magazine, first published in 1922.

CHRISTMAS GOES COMMERCIAL

Take Us to Gamages!

As long as there have been merchants selling their wares, there have been opportunities to boast about their products. And what better reason to build up stock, advertise goods and encourage customers to open their pocketbooks just a little farther than the season of giving? Large department stores have often used the festive season to put extra effort into keeping their patrons lingering in their store aisles longer than usual by building a Christmas village, a winter wonderland or—as in the case of London's Gamages—an enchanted castle for youngsters and their families to wander through and capture the spirit of the season. In the 1923 edition of *Good Housekeeping* magazine,

 Gamages called for boys and girls from far and wide to meet Jolly Old Santa at the gates of his "enchanted castle." There, youngsters were promised they would "explore the Battlements and the Dungeons, the Baronial Hall—a veritable Aladdin's Cave of gorgeous things direct from Fairyland."

Mincemeat Magic

In 1924, *Good Housekeeping* magazine guaranteed absolute satisfaction with anything and everything advertised within its pages and a recipe for "Homemade Mincemeat"—one of almost 100 taste-tested recipes put out in a booklet by Hugon & Co., Ltd.—was no exception. Along with the traditional candied peel of lemon and orange, raisins and currants, Hugon's "Atora—The Good Beef Suet" was a main ingredient.

What Any Woman Wants?

Throughout the 1920s, Britain's *Good Housekeeping* magazine encouraged men everywhere to buy the women in their lives any of a number of cleaning gadgets. The best of the day, in 1924 anyway, was the British-made Whirlwind Suction Sweeper. The carpet-cleaning contraption used nothing more than a "monthly sip of oil" to keep it in running order. No electricity required. And woe to the woman whose husband and children hadn't ensured that this perfect gift found its way beneath their family Christmas tree. The full-page advertisement made it clear that "A Home Without a Whirlwind is a Home for Dust."

Little Toy Trains

Good Housekeeping had something for everyone in the pages of its 1927 Christmas edition. And in case the little lad in your life had yet to make it clear that the *Hornby Book of Trains* would be the perfect Christmas gift, Hornby Trains took out a large advertisement in the magazine saying their 1927–28 edition was the best ever. Not only did the book outline the history of the locomotive, it provided page upon page of colored photos, illustrations and price information on the company's trains, rolling stock and accessories.

Christmas Dinner

What were some people enjoying for Christmas dinner in 1929? One menu suggested by the Good Housekeeping Institute in Strand, England, included "Chestnut Soup, Poached Plaice, Roast Turkey with Stuffing, Boiled Ham, Bread Sauce, Brussels Sprouts, Roast Potatoes, Christmas Pudding with Foamy Brandy Sauce, Mince Pies and Peter Pan Christmas Pudding."

The December 1897 issue of the *Ladies' Home Journal* highlighted the following menu: "Oysters on the half shell, Clear Soup, Custard and Spinach Blocks, Deviled spaghetti, Roast Turkey & Chestnut Stuffing, Sweet-Potato Croquettes, Peas in Turnip Cups, Ginger Sherbet, Lettuce Salad Cheese Balls, Toasted Crackers, Plum Pudding & Hard Sauce and Coffee Bonbons."

DID YOU  KNOW?

Cutting and decorating that fine Christmas tree find is one of those festive activities that propels most folk into the spirit of the season. But just like your pet pooch, it needs its daily drink of water. In fact, maintaining a healthy Christmas tree could take a quart of water a day.

Digestive Aids

If you needed help digesting Christmas dinner in 1929, *Good Housekeeping* magazine advertised Fox's Glacier Mints "for a digestive Xmas." Apparently, the mints were "so seductive, so refreshing, so delicious, so cooling; they are a great temptation." As always, *Good Housekeeping* stood by their advertisements, stating "Advertised Goods are Good Goods."

Gift Certificates

The 1960 edition of *Good Housekeeping* suggested a gift voucher from Harrods in Knightsbridge or from any other major department store as "heaven to receive because you have the joy of opening it on Christmas morning and the joy of buying anything you like with it on one of those dull January days when Christmas seems months away."

Mele Kalikimaka
in Hawaiian

Christmas Today
and Tomorrow

For Christmas to remain relevant, it must evolve with society. As one editorial writer put it, while many complain of the commercialization of Christmas, few recognize that it is because of that commercialization that Christmas has gained the popularity it has.

And so, new traditions are formed. Some traditions, such as sending Christmas cards, are meant to quietly spread good cheer between friends and family, especially those living far away. Others, such as piecing together a collection of food and gift items for the less fortunate, are more visible ways a community can work together to spread Christmas cheer.

Unfortunately, though they are wonderful additions to the festive fare of today, where and how some of these new traditions, such as Secret Santa, began isn't clear.

So if you or your community comes up with something new to celebrate the season, don't forget to document it. Who knows, someone else might pick up on your idea and years from now people will be reading about your Christmas contribution.

NEW TRADITIONS

Why Boxing Day, Anyway?

Strictly speaking, and according to the *Merriam-Webster Dictionary*, Boxing Day is the "first weekday after Christmas." Nothing is ever as simple as it seems, and the origin of Boxing Day is no exception. In fact, most of the western world refers to the day after Christmas as Boxing Day, so even Merriam-Webster's definition isn't written in stone, as it were.

As for the origin of this day, one source points to the centuries-old practice of merchants and other wealthier folk packing food and fruits in boxes to give to their servants as a Christmas gift of sorts. Apparently, there was also a time in Britain when workers would bring boxes to work the day after Christmas, hoping their employers were in proper seasonal spirits and would fill them up with money and other goodies. Another story says that Boxing Day came from the practice of opening the church's donation box on Christmas and doling out the money to the poor folk of the neighborhood the following day.

Either way, if you're a shopaholic, the origin of Boxing Day isn't nearly as important as the current retail practice of slashing prices that day in a last-ditch effort to boost annual sales and clear the way for spring stock!

Season's Greetings

The tradition of giving Christmas cards is a relatively modern one, originating just 150 years ago in jolly old England. The story goes that in 1843, Sir Henry Cole asked his good friend and artist, John Calcott Horsley, for a favor. There were so many people Sir Henry wanted to send season's greetings to and just not enough time to write and post letters to all of them. He was also very concerned about the plight of the poor and thought that at such a special time of the year, people who were able to should make every effort to share their abundance.

This is where John Calcott Horsley came in. What if he painted a card that illustrated the feeding and clothing of the poor? Sir Henry could have the card replicated and send cards out to all of his friends!

As the old saying goes, the road to hell is paved with good intentions, and after the first Christmas card was published, it met with harsh criticism. The reason why had to do with John Calcott Horsley's image of a happy family celebrating the season, which seemed innocent enough. However, a youngster was shown enjoying a sip of wine, and this offended the sensibilities of the prim and proper British folk. John Calcott Horsley was corrupting the minds of little children, they argued.

The outrage so deeply upset Sir Henry that, according to legend, he declined to give out cards the following year.

Regardless of the controversy, sending out Christmas cards became a hit. Most were inscribed with a greeting of some sort or other. This greeting from a card of the late 1800s is quite elaborate:

> *May Christmas bring you all pure and perfect happiness.*
> *To you, like birds, my wishes wing their way singing,*
> *with naught to mar their warmth and lightness,*
> *may purest pleasures crown your Christmas Day*
> *and make your home a scene of love and brightness.*

Not all Christmas cards of the day were so sentimental. Some cards sported squeaking mechanisms, while pop-up cards displayed intricate, three-dimensional scenes. Trick cards offered something unexpected, such as the pretend banknotes on one joke card that looked so real they had to be pulled from circulation.

It's likely that American settlers receiving Christmas cards from family back home started the tradition in the western world. To meet the need, merchants had to import cards from England until 1875. That's when a German immigrant named Louis Prang established a lithograph shop and produced the first American-made Christmas cards. Business was so good that by 1881, Prang must have been a very wealthy man, since by then he was producing and selling more than five million cards each year.

Good Old Mrs. Claus

We all know that behind every good man is a good woman—or so the saying goes. And though we didn't hear about his missus until the mid 20th century, obviously Santa Claus is no exception.

Mrs. Santa Claus made her debut in modern society in 1956. That's when British-born composer George Melachrino penned the song "Mrs. Santa Claus."

At least one movie has been dedicated to Santa's right-hand lady. It is called—you guessed it—*Mrs. Santa Claus* and stars Angela

Lansbury as the jolly lead character. It debuted on television screens across North America in 1996.

Today, Mrs. Claus can be seen in malls throughout North America, dutifully assisting her husband in bringing Christmas cheer to youngsters.

DID YOU  **KNOW?**

Every year, the U.S. lights its National Christmas Tree in Washington, DC. And though temperatures may not dip into the deep-freeze range that some parts of Canada face, it usually feels like Christmas. But not in 1984. When the tree lights flashed on for the first time that Christmas, temperatures were in the 70s Fahrenheit. It may not have been sweltering hot, but it was definitely one of the warmest tree lightings in history.

The Longest Night

While most of the world that celebrates Christmas is gearing up for holiday festivities for many weeks before the big day, many people find themselves struggling with trauma, grief, pain or some type of loss.

The Longest Night, the Blue Christmas, the Service of Remembrance—whatever the name, many Christian churches have taken to holding a special service for those who are struggling with personal issues and find it difficult to deal with all the festivities of the season.

Typically held some time during Advent—the four weeks leading up to Christmas—the service offers hope and comfort, prayer and meditation, strength and support to those who attend. While some churches host this type of service on their own, a number of churches in an area may join forces and hold a single, larger event for an entire community.

Christmas Seals

It all began with a Danish postman named Einar Holboell. And to say the tireless worker, sorting an unending pile of Christmas mail one cold December night in Denmark in 1903, was soft-hearted is an understatement.

The story goes that while Einar was working, he happened to notice a small boy and girl, threadbare and cold and obviously poor, wander past his office window. He was saddened at the sight, thinking that this season of plenty should be for the greater good of all, not just the benefit of a few!

Looking at the vast amount of mail before him, he reasoned that just one extra stamp on each letter would add up to a considerable amount, to be sure. The idea intrigued him so much that he started fine-tuning it as soon as the Christmas rush was over.

He must have been a mighty fine salesman, since his enthusiasm spread to King Christian IX, who added just a tiny little suggestion of his own. What better way to endorse the idea of Christmas Seals, the king reasoned, than to have a picture of his own dear wife, Queen Louise, on the first installment? The postman must have agreed, because that's exactly what happened, and in 1904, the first year they went on sale, more than four million Christmas seals were sold.

Apparently, fundraising of any sort wasn't popular at that time in Denmark, and the next challenge in this exciting adventure was determining how to distribute the money raised. It was eventually decided that the children who were in the most distress were the hundreds, even perhaps thousands, who suffered from tuberculosis. Two years worth of Christmas Seals sales went to the building of two hospitals "for the treatment of tuberculos children."

Seeing the success of this idea, Norway and Sweden started similar programs of their own, and by 1907, the idea had spread to North America, where a sanatorium in Delaware was in danger of closing because it couldn't raise a much-needed $300. Should this happen, patients infected with tuberculosis would be let out into the general public and spread the disease! Dr. Joseph P. Wales shared his concerns with his cousin, Emily Bissell. Having heard of the Christmas Seal program from a Danish American friend named Jacob Riis, she proposed they try the idea themselves.

The American public didn't like linking a disease to the Christmas season, so they didn't initially buy into it, but Emily wasn't discouraged. She marched over to the daily paper and asked the news editor for some publicity for the cause. He refused, but a chance encounter with a columnist got her the ear of the managing editor and the slogan "Stamp out tuberculosis" was born.

Canadians picked up on the Christmas Seal campaign the following year. Boosted by daily stories in the *Toronto Globe*, interest grew. Soon, folks throughout Canada were getting involved. School children in Toronto sold Christmas Seals, staff at the *Regina Leader* sold Christmas Seals, Rev. G.A. Moore of Saint John, New Brunswick, organized his parishioners to sell Christmas Seals. The enthusiasm for raising money to "Stamp out tuberculosis" was almost as contagious as the disease itself. And by 1927, the Canadian Tuberculosis Association had opted to adopt Christmas Seals as their main method of raising money.

Although tuberculosis is under control today, there are still 3000 cases a year in Canada and over 14,000 in the United States. Over the years, the Canadian Tuberculosis Association evolved into the Canadian Lung Association, and Christmas Seals are still used as a fundraiser, but their focus has now expanded to include all lung diseases.

The Kettle Campaign

Rare is the person who hasn't at least once in their lifetime come across a man or woman, often dressed in an official uniform complete with starched white gloves and bell in hand, standing beside a hanging glass globe (known as a kettle) filled with bits of change and an assortment of bills.

The Salvation Army Christmas Kettle campaign is one of the most well-known Christmas fundraising efforts of modern time. Each year, officers of the Christian organization gather themselves and volunteers to stand at store entryways across the world, hoping that those who can will favor them with a donation. And from that first kettle collection back in 1891 to this very day, the money is used to feed the hungry, provide grocery certificates to the needy, assist those struck down by disaster and generally help society wherever possible.

Salvation Army Captain Joseph McFee, struggling to figure out a way to provide a Christmas dinner for the poor in San Francisco, is credited with establishing the program as it is today. The idea sprang from a memory he had, when as a sailor in Liverpool, England, he had seen a large pot, called "Simpson's Pot," into which passersby deposited charitable donations.

The cause for which those donations were being collected seems to be lost in history, but McFee got permission to set up a collection pot of his own, and the poor of his area were blessed with a Christmas feast that year. News of his success spread to other Salvation Army corps, and by 1895, as many as 30 of them were on board with the program.

While neighbors can often more readily understand an idea, especially after seeing it firsthand, taking it father afield can be challenging. When Officer William A. McIntyre introduced the kettle collection idea to his colleagues in Boston in 1897, it wasn't favorably received. After all, standing on a street corner like that was akin to begging, some reasoned.

Not so easily deterred, Officer McIntyre, his wife and his sister set up three kettles in Boston's city center. Between the Boston

efforts and those of San Francisco, more than 150,000 less-fortunate folk received a Christmas dinner that year.

Today, more than 100 years later, some parts of the collection process have changed, but most have remained the same. Officers still man the collection, which has transformed from a black kettle to a glass globe, but so do volunteers and other staff members. According to one report, a little glitz and glam—such as a "self-ringing bell or a booth complete with public-address system to broadcast the traditional Christmas carols"—have been added in some locations. And with the help of the annual media hoopla, the campaign receives a lot of attention. Even folks who can't afford large donations feel good about the dollar or two they can drop into the pot.

Perhaps the success of the program stems from its eternal value, the true meaning of Christmas—peace on earth and goodwill to all people.

DID YOU  KNOW?

Santa has occasionally had a hard time. The political powers that be in England banned Christmas from 1649 to 1660. In 1918, the U.S. Congress actually considered canceling Christmas, and in the 1950s, clerics in the country of France took it upon themselves to burn Santa in effigy! Why be so hard on the poor guy? It was thought that Santa depicted a bastardization of Saint Nicholas and took the focus away from the true meaning of Christmas, as did the perceived commercialization of Christmas.

Anonymous Giving

Let's see, there's Secret Santa, Santa's Elves, Santa's Anonymous, Christmas Elves, Santa's Toy Box, the Christmas Hamper Program, the Christmas Gift Certificate Fund—and those are just the names I can pull from the top of my head! Each of these names represents a community's Christmas season anonymous-giving program. It's not clear where or when the first such programs began, but in keeping with the spirit of the season, you'll be hard-pressed to find a community that doesn't have its own traditions for collecting toys and money for the less fortunate.

MITHO MAKOSI KESIKANSI
in Cree

Christianity and Christmas

But the angel said to them, "Do not be afraid. I bring you good news of great joy that will be for all the people. Today, in the town of David, a Savior has been born to you; he is Christ the Lord. This will be a sign to you: You will find a baby wrapped in cloths and lying in a manger."

– Luke 2:10–12

Although, at times, different churches squabble over doctrine, this big event—the birth of Christ heralded at Christmastime by people around the world—is the foundation of the Christian faith. It is a story of a little baby bringing hope and joy. It is a story of forgiveness and reconciliation. It is a story of peace on earth and goodwill to all.

DAYS OF THE CHRISTIAN CALENDAR

A Day for Adam and Eve

Today, Christmas Eve serves as a preamble for the big event— Christmas Day. But for Christians living in medieval times, it was a day set aside for a special acknowledgment. Known as Adam and Eve Day, earth's first man and wife were initially celebrated as saints, of sorts, by Christians in the Middle East, Eastern Europe and North Africa.

The reason for choosing Christmas Eve as the day for this celebration was intricate, to say the least. Early theologians often drew parallels between Adam and Eve and Jesus and Mary. They believed that through their obedience, Jesus and the Virgin Mary saved humanity from the disobedience of Adam and Eve. The Bible itself draws a similar comparison, referring to Jesus as the "second Adam."

Although early Christians considered Adam and Eve to be the mother and father of all people, the two were never made saints by the Roman Catholic Church, and the tradition of Adam and Eve Day was never formally adopted by the Church proper. Still, the annual remembrance, complete with feasting and a mystery play retelling the Genesis story, continued until the Church banned such events in the 15th century. Today, the only remnant of this early tradition can be found in some of the Eastern Orthodox traditions, particularly the Greek Orthodox Church, which honors Adam and Eve on the Sunday before Christmas.

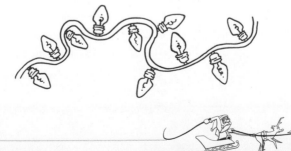

A Wreath of Candles

The four Sundays leading up to Christmas are called Advent in the Christian church. Stemming from the Latin *advenire*, the word Advent means "to come towards."

Traditionally, these four weeks are not unlike the days of Lent— they are a time of reflection, penance and preparation for the celebration of Christ's birth. Depending on the particular Christian tradition adhered to, fasting is quite common. The Biblical verses assigned to the church reading calendar for those days speak of the promise of a coming messiah and the need to prepare the way for Christ on earth and in our hearts. Church hymns sung during Advent also echo these messages.

As a means of providing followers with a concrete, outward sign of the journey through the season, the custom of the Advent wreath was developed in northern Europe. A collection of greenery was arranged into the shape of a wreath, a continuous circle that symbolized the promise of eternal life through Christ. This wreath was then secured to a flat surface and four candles were spaced equal distances apart around the wreath. Originally, three of these candles were purple, to stand for penance, and the fourth candle was pink, representing the coming joy of Christmas. The tradition varies at times, depending on the church. Sometimes three red candles are used, representing the blood of Christ, with a single white candle to symbolize Christ's purity.

Either way, each Sunday, one more candle is lit and a prayer said, reminding the faithful of the journey that Advent is meant to be. Two of the three purple candles are traditionally lit first. Then the pink candle is lit on the third Sunday of Advent, also known as Mary Sunday or Rose Sunday, because in Catholic tradition, Mary was referred to as the "Rose." The readings for this Sunday focus on the Annunciation of Mary. This was when the angel Gabriel visited Mary and told her she would conceive a son and he would be called Jesus. Because of the foretelling of the birth of Christ, this pink candle also stands as a reminder that though the church is still in darkness, "there is hope and the light of Christ is coming." The last purple candle is lit on the fourth Sunday of Advent, and a more recent North American tradition has added a central white candle that is lit on Christmas Day to represent the light of Christ.

DID YOU KNOW?

According to a 2001 study, the average shopping mall Santa weighs in at 218 pounds.

Saint Basil the Great

While most of us, Christian or not, know of Saint Nicholas, not many associate Saint Basil the Great with Christmas. For the Greek Orthodox Church and practitioners of that denomination, the Christmas season can't be celebrated without homage being paid to this revered saint.

Basil the Great was the Bishop of Caesarea. He was born in the then-Greek province of Cappadocia (currently part of Turkey) and lived from 330 to 379 AD, becoming known as one of the great leaders of the church. But he wasn't one for glory. Instead, Basil spent his life caring for the sick, the orphaned and the poor.

One particularly touching legend about Saint Basil revolves around him giving to the poor without their even suspecting it. As the story goes, Basil noticed there were a large number of poor families in one village. In an effort to keep them from feeling humiliated by his generosity, Basil approached the village baker, handed him a sack of coins and asked that he insert one in every loaf he baked. That way, when the villagers purchased the bread and found the coins, they'd feel they'd been blessed with good fortune. This legend is the basis for the New Year's Day tradition of the *Vasilopita*, or Basil's bread.

While Saint Nicholas doesn't bring presents for Greek youngsters as he is said to do in other parts of the world, Saint Basil the Great is blessed with that honor in Greece. Also known as a patron saint of children, he performs this act of giving not on Christmas Eve, but on New Year's Eve—and Greek youngsters anticipate his arrival like children from other countries anticipate Saint Nicholas. It naturally follows that Saint Basil's Day, the day set aside as his feast day, is January 1.

Ritual Blessings

The Greek tradition called the "Blessing of the Water" takes place throughout Greece every January 5 and 6, the Eve of Epiphany and Epiphany. There are two parts to this tradition— the Lesser Blessing and the Greater Blessing—and the ritual is similar for both. A priest, a tree branch, a cross and, of course, water are all necessary elements in each ceremony. In the Lesser Blessing, which is held on January 5, the Holy Spirit is asked to bless the water, a prayer is said, and then the priest dips a cross into the water three times to symbolize the baptism of Jesus in the River Jordan. The priest then dips a sprig of basil or a small evergreen branch into the water, and for those gathered who would like a blessing, the priest touches the wet branch to their foreheads, saying *"Chronia polla"* or "Good year." Participants are then given a vial of holy water to use at home throughout the year.

While the Lesser Blessing usually takes place in the church, the Greater Blessing is often held beside the ocean or another natural body of water. For this blessing, the priest and congregation proceed to the water. Again, the priest blesses the water, but this time, instead of dipping a small cross, he tosses a large one into the depths of the water. At that precise moment, the church bells peal, wildly decorated boats appear as if out of nowhere, and young men dive into the water in an effort to retrieve the cross. The lucky man who manages this feat is formally blessed and has earned himself good luck for the following year.

DID YOU  KNOW?

The State of Indiana has a town named in honor of Santa Claus.

The Feast of Stephen

The Feast of Stephen, which takes place on December 26 for Christians in the West and on December 27 for those in the East, commemorates Saint Stephen—the first martyr of the Christian church. Charged with blasphemy because he was spreading the teachings of Christ, which were felt to be in direct opposition to the Law of Moses, Stephen was stoned to death by a mob led by Paul before his conversion to Christianity.

For the folks in Ireland, Saint Stephen's Day is a national holiday. But instead of a more focused, reflective period such as that typically spent during the weeks of Advent and on Christmas Eve and Christmas Day, Saint Stephen's Day is the first of the 12 days of Christmas and a time when the Irish let loose and have a little fun.

Sretan Bozic

in Croatian

Hearth and Home

Getting the home ready for Christmas has traditionally meant a thorough scrubbing, the spicy scent of ginger and cinnamon and the flicker of candles decorating a dining table or a Yule log burning in the fireplace. Holly, ivy, Christmas linens, jingle bells—all this and so much more is commonplace in households that celebrate the season. So where did these traditions come from?

Humans are such an interesting lot. I'm not sure if it's because we bore easily, if we are simply very creative or if we just like putting our own stamp on things. Either way, while a tradition might originate in one country, as soon as it moves to another, it has likely undergone several adaptations. Occasionally, more than one country claims to have created a particular custom. And though they can spar all they want, history isn't always clear, either.

So if you're looking for a new idea for decorating the family home, you may want to try one or two of the ideas listed below—or perhaps you might want to adapt an idea to suit your own purposes and start yet another Christmas tradition.

TRADITIONS AND TREATS

Aussie Light Show

Put away the holly and the mistletoe and make room for wattle flowers, bottle brush and *Ceratopetalum gummiferum*. When it comes to decorating the family home, Aussies have an ample array of seasonal foliage to choose from. A kookaburra bird in a eucalyptus wreath is just one example of a uniquely Australian decoration. Still, electric lights and artificial Christmas trees are appearing more and more often in Aussie homes. Back in 1998, Aussie resident Len Doof was thought to have the largest private Christmas light show in the world, with more than 47,000 lights shining for all to see. Bet that cost a fortune in electricity bills!

Although the jury may still be out on the "world's largest" declaration, Len Doof continues to bring his version of the light of Christmas to anyone passing by his marvelous display.

A Patriotic Christmas

Red and white are the colors of the Danish flag and are used extensively in Denmark when decorating for the Christmas season. Woven hearts made of red and white paper are favorite Danish symbols. Families gather to create these festive hearts, which are then used as tree ornaments or mobiles. The red and white theme continues with the creation of garlands made by joining dozens and dozens of handcrafted, miniature Danish flags. Talk about patriotism at its finest!

Mabuhay! Live Life to the Full!

The people of the Philippines, a country known as the "Land of Fiestas," really know how to live their greeting of *Mabuhay!* and Christmas in the Philippines is the biggest fiesta of the year. A deeply religious country, Christian observances of all kinds are front and center during the Christmas season. But the people of the Philippines love color in all areas of their lives. From personal adornments to seasonal decorations, there are splashes of color

everywhere. Even the Filipino *jeepneys*, elongated jeep-like vehicles that are used for public transportation, are decked out with seasonal adornments. So it's no surprise that color plays a big role in that country's Christmas traditions.

Large, elaborate and, of course, colorful star lanterns called *parol* are a feature decoration in most Filipino homes. There's no disguising the significance behind the adornment—a lighted star can represent nothing other than the star of Bethlehem. Although the symbolism of the *parol* appears in traditions around the world, this ornament is unique to the Philippines. Families often gather together to create simple star lanterns made from strips of balsa wood secured together and covered with tissue paper. These homemade efforts are usually about 10 inches wide. But custom-made lanterns can come in all sizes. More elaborate versions can be made of hemp, beads, shells or other material, even colorful pieces of glass welded together and backlit for a stunning effect, especially at night. These are often purchased from artisans in open-air marketplaces.

The lantern capital of the Philippines is said to be the province of Pampanga, where giant lanterns weighing over 2000 pounds and measuring 40 feet in diameter are constructed by master craftsmen. Once completed, these *parol* are, of course, lit with thousands of lights, creating a colorful spectacle not seen anywhere else in the world.

DID YOU KNOW?

The use of oil in cooking specialty dishes such as *latkes* (potato pancakes) is of special significance during Hanukkah. It is a reminder of the eight days and nights that just one day's supply of oil burned in the original miracle.

Paper, Paper Everywhere

Paper plays a huge role in the traditional tree decorations of Germany. One of the most popular ornaments is an origami-like, 16-pointed, two-tone ribbon star. These stars, which can also be made out of strips of paper and dipped in wax to firm up the finished product, are created by interlocking four ribbons of equal length to form a basket-weave foundation. Then the paper ribbons are folded to form a star with 16 points. A thin thread is sewn through the ribbon between two of the star's points, and then the star is hung. I've had the opportunity to create the paper-and-wax version of this intricate little star, and believe me, it took hours! Even with a steady, practiced hand, making enough of these stars to cover a tree would be no small feat!

Other paper decorations include a pleated paper star and, believe it or not, at least three different variations of a paper bell!

Edible Candleholders

In order to ensure there was always a candle burning on the windowsill, the Irish came up with a unique decorating tradition to deal with the lack of actual candleholders. They improvised using, what else—a turnip!

They simply sliced off the turnip greens, along with a portion of the top of the turnip, sliced the rooted bottom to flatten it and cored a hole in the center to fit the candle—*voilá*, a candleholder! Of course, I'm not sure anyone would want to eat the turnip after it became coated in wax during the Christmas season.

DID YOU KNOW?

In our 24-hour-a-day, seven-day-a-week, information-overloaded society, television stations in Iceland actually shut down for a few hours every Christmas Eve.

Bells, Bells, Bells...

I heard the bells on Christmas day,
Their old familiar carols play,
And wild and sweet the words repeat
Of peace on earth, goodwill to men.

Composed by Henry W. Longfellow in 1864, "I Heard the Bells on Christmas Day" is a favorite traditional carol of the season—and one of a great many bell-themed hymns. There's "Jingle Bells" and "Jingle Bell Rock," "Carol of the Bells" and "Silver Bells." And there's a plethora of other Christmas carols in which bells play a significant role. "Ding Dong Merrily on High" is just one example. But what is so significant about bells that they have managed to capture our interest so completely?

From their first use in ancient China 4000 years ago, bells have played both a symbolic role as well as a utilitarian role. Stone cuttings dating back to the fourth century BC depict Alexander the Great's war charioteers having adorned their horses with bells. Moses adorned the hem of the newly ordained Aaron with bells so that when he met with the Lord in the Holy of Holies he would not die (Exodus 28:33–35). Bells were even used in pagan winter celebrations to frighten off evil spirits in the night.

Saint Paulinus, Bishop of Nola, Italy, is credited as the first to use bells in the Christian church in the fourth century. Today, bells are used as decorations on the Christmas tree, to cheer on the newly married, to welcome high noon or to announce a blessed event—as ZuZu Bailey explains to her father George in the movie *It's a Wonderful Life*: "Every time a bell rings, an angel gets his wings."

DID YOU KNOW?

It is the sole responsibility of the North American Aerospace Defense Command, otherwise known as NORAD, to track Santa's journey on Christmas Eve.

Be My Teddy Bear

It's historically considered one of the most requested gifts of all time, but did you ever wonder how the teddy bear came to be? The story has to do with President Theodore Roosevelt, a dispute between Mississippi and Louisiana and a bear hunt.

In November 1902, President Roosevelt successfully settled a border dispute between the states of Mississippi and Louisiana. Hearing that the hunting was pretty good, the president decided to take a little time for himself and set off on a bear hunt. Although he and his entourage didn't find any bears, one of his party captured and tied up a bear cub, offering it to the president to shoot. Instead of being thrilled, President Roosevelt was appalled by the gesture. What sport was there in shooting an exhausted, confined animal? He ordered that the bear cub be released.

Cartoonist Clifford Barryman immortalized the scene with a sketch that later appeared on the front page of the *Washington Post*. Using the idea as a retail opportunity, a shopkeeper named Morris Michtom from Brooklyn, New York, had his wife make two stuffed toy bears using a soft, plush fabric and finished off with black, shoe-button eyes. He posed the bears in his shop window, and it wasn't long before it was clear they'd be a fast favorite as gifts for the Christmas season.

Coincidentally, the Steiff Company of Giengen, Germany, began to manufacture similar stuffed bears. And the rest, as they say, is retail history.

The Story of Stockings

The stockings were hung by the chimney with care...

The question is, why were they placed there?

There are several legends about how the hanging of Christmas stockings for Santa Claus to fill with goodies originated, but the favorite seems connected directly with Saint Nicholas, Bishop of Myra, himself.

The story goes that a wealthy nobleman was heartbroken over the death of his wife. Not thinking clearly and in the pit of depression, he squandered his fortune. His financial ruin meant a life of spinsterhood for his three daughters, since they no longer had dowries with which to acquire husbands.

Having heard the local gossip on the matter as he was passing through their village, the goodhearted Nicholas wanted to help.

He knew the father would reject a direct gift of money, so Nicholas decided to climb up to the rooftop in the dead of night and drop three bags of gold down the family's chimney. As luck would have it, the daughters had done their weekly washing that day and had each hung their stockings on the fireplace mantle to dry. They woke to find dry stockings and a dowry for each of them! Once others heard the story, it doesn't take a genius to figure out that they, too, decided to see if they would be as lucky! And so, another tradition was born.

While it's likely the custom spread to North America via European settlers, Clement Clark Moore is traditionally credited with spreading its popularity.

Who, you ask? Well, you may not recall his name, but you likely have at least some of the words of his famous poem memorized:

> *The stockings were hung by the chimney with care,*
> *In hopes that Saint Nicholas soon would be there.*

DID YOU KNOW?

The image of Santa Claus brings Christmas to mind in a heartbeat, but did you know his image has also been used to sell all manner of merchandise, including soap, whiskey and Scotch tape.

Mistletoe

The story of mistletoe dates back to 200 years before the birth of Christ and definitely has roots in the pagan faith of druidism.

The scientific name of this plant is *Viscum album*, and though it is an evergreen, it roots and grows on the branches of deciduous trees. An overabundance of this parasite on a tree can kill the host, but instead of seeing mistletoe as an infestation, the fact that it survived and thrived led to it being revered as a symbol of strength and eternal life by ancient Romans. The Romans were said to drop their weapoms and embrace their enemies when meeting under the mistletoe. And one legend links the plant to the Scandinavian goddess of love, Frigga. The story surrounding Frigga is dark and sad and results in the death of her son and husband, so it's hard to see where the love is in this legend. Still, at some point in Scandinavian history, the mistletoe went from being a weapon used for evil to a sign of love and goodwill.

The tradition of kissing under the mistletoe takes the story to—where else—jolly old England. Apparently the rather reserved British of today were a little less so in days gone by. It seems the English used to give visitors a kiss when greeting them or saying farewell. Somehow, sometime in the 18th century, this custom transformed into the Christmas practice of kissing under the mistletoe.

The tradition continued to mutate, as it were, depending on where the kissing took place. One legend tells of how a young man could have as many kisses under the mistletoe as there were berries on the bough. With each kiss, a berry was to be removed, and when they were all gone, he was out of luck. Season of love or not, there'd be no more kissing for him, no siree!

Today, festive folks who like to hang mistletoe in their homes aren't nearly as stringent with the number of kisses allowed. After all, even if you were able to pluck the plastic berries, chances are the whole thing would fall apart!

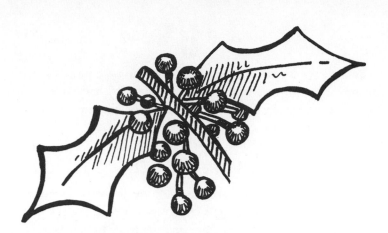

The Holly and the Ivy

Another tradition with pagan origins intricately tied to the celebration of the winter solstice, the holly and ivy have been used as Christmas decorations for centuries and have even adopted Christian significance.

Originally, these two plants were chosen for winter solstice celebrations because they typically looked their best in the dead of winter, brightening up the dismal season with vibrant greens and the holly's red berries. They also had the job of warding off evil spirits. When these plants were adopted into Christian Christmas traditions, the church created a Christian significance for them. Hence, the holly's red berries came to symbolize the blood of Jesus shed at the crucifixion and the thorny leaves came to represent the crown of thorns He wore.

In order to grow, ivy needs to lean against something solid. Therefore, the ivy came to represent our need to cling to God for support in our lives.

DID YOU KNOW?

The holly was believed to be a male plant and the ivy, a female plant. Apparently, it was once believed that whichever of the two was first brought into the home during the Christmas season signified which partner would rule the roost that year.

Bûche de Noël

The Yule log is part of Christmas tradition in many countries. In some cultures, a large log is chosen on Candlemas, the final feast of Christmas for some Christian faiths. Candlemas is usually celebrated on February 2, so the Yule log is chosen almost a full year before it will be lit on Christmas Eve or Christmas morning. The reason for cutting it so far in advance is to let the wood dry, resulting in a more even burning during the Christmas season. In other cultures, the Yule log is cut on Christmas Eve, while others are more particular about the type of log cut, insisting it be taken from a green oak or even a beech tree.

Once the Yule log is lit, it must burn for a minimum of 12 hours or, if possible, all 12 days of Christmas. The fire was supposed to ward off evil or, in some customs, protect the home from witchcraft. Ashes from the Yule log fire were often kept and tossed over a farmer's field to ensure a good crop or dropped in a family's water source to purify the water. Sometimes a piece from the current year's Yule log was kept and used to light the Yule log the following year.

But for the family whose Yule log went out before the mandatory 12 hours was up, bad luck would be a constant threat throughout the New Year.

While the tradition of the Yule log isn't as commonly practiced as it once was, some countries have made innovative adjustments to fit modern life. It was in France, for example, that the log-shaped cake called the *bûche de Noël* was created. Today, Christmas logs, which are made in both cake and ice cream varieties, are a common seasonal treat in homes in France and elsewhere.

DID YOU KNOW?

While Argentinean families participate in the tradition of decorating a Christmas tree, they don't limit themselves to the evergreen variety. Any tree is suitable for decorating in that country—live or artificial.

The Red Leaves of Christmas

The poinsettia is a native Mexican plant, and though its place in Christmas tradition in that country stems as far back as the 17th century, when Franciscan monks were known to use the plants in their annual celebrations, it wasn't always part of the Christmas tradition in other parts of North America.

Known by a number of names, including Mexican Flame Leaf, Christmas Star, Noche Buena—or, going back to its scientific name, as *Euphorbia pulcherrima*—the popular Christmas plant wasn't called a poinsettia until 1828, when Joel R. Poinsett, U.S. ambassador to Mexico, brought one to the United States during his travels between the two countries.

The story attached to this tradition bears a striking resemblance to the plight of the little drummer boy. In this story, a young child (sometimes it's a boy, sometimes a girl, depending on the variation) is on her way to church one Christmas Eve and realizes she doesn't have a gift for baby Jesus. Instead of giving the gift of music as the little drummer boy did, the little girl in this legend collects an assortment of green branches as she makes her way to church. At the time, the branches appear to be nothing more than weeds. Still, having been taught that honoring Christ with what we have is the most important part of any gift, she brings her humble offering into the church.

Now, were you to see a poinsettia in the wild, you'd likely be struck by its wild and unruly appearance and think it badly in need of pruning. But for the parishioners of that Christmas Eve, the collection of branches and leaves was said to have bloomed beneath their eyes as many luscious, red, star-shaped "flowers" appeared and everyone gathered believed they had witnessed a miracle.

DID YOU KNOW?

Ninety-eight percent of live Christmas trees adorning homes for the festive season are grown on tree farms.

The Elves of Christmas

Thanks to fairy tales such as *Snow White and the Seven Dwarfs* or stories of Santa Claus and his entourage of elfin creatures, most people in the western world think elves are helpful, kind, caring and even sweet. But elves actually first appeared in German mythology. And though they were often thought to possess magical powers, they weren't always nice. Some elves could be downright nasty, cause illness and even give people bad dreams. In fact, a German word for nightmare is *alpdrucken*, which means "elf-pressure."

DID YOU KNOW?

Elf-believing folk in Denmark say that only cats can see elves. So if your kitty gets spooked for no apparent reason, perhaps you have an elf or two lurking in your house.

Sweet Treats on the Tree

Blueberry, cherry, cinnamon, even Irish cream. Today, candy canes come in so many variations, it's hard to remember all the flavor options. But when the confectionary treat first made an appearance in Christmas tradition back in the 17th century, the plain, unflavored sugar canes came only in one color—white.

The crook-shaped candy we know today came from the Cologne Cathedral in Germany courtesy of one particularly innovative choirmaster. Those first candies were handed out to youngsters of the parish to occupy them and keep them quiet during the church's Christmas ceremonies. When other churches heard of the idea, they also took to passing out the "candy crooks," and before long, the candy cane custom had spread across Europe.

The idea of using candy canes as tree decorations was first introduced in the United States in 1847 by a German Swedish immigrant named August Imgard. It's obvious, then, that they were available in the U.S. But they must have either been imported or handmade, since as recently as the 1920s, Bob McCormack was credited with having been the first American to have pulled and twisted the first candy canes into crook shapes for family and friends. Since the process was so time consuming and labor intensive, McCormack only made a limited number.

By the 1950s, McCormack's brother-in-law, a Catholic priest named Gregory Keller, had given the custom a firm foundation in society by developing and building the first equipment able to mass produce these sweet treats. Today, about 1.8 million candy canes are produced each year in the U.S.— enough to span the distance between Santa Claus, Indiana, and North Pole, Arkansas, 32 times!

It's not clear when the red stripe was added to the white candy cane. One source points to Christmas cards as a measuring stick, explaining that candy canes in pre-1900 cards are depicted as a solid white, while those after the turn of the 20th century show a solid red ribbon running through them, along with three  thin stripes. It is thought that the ribbon was added to represent the blood of Christ of the Easter story, and one interpretation of the three thin stripes is that they represent the Holy Trinity. The white background is said to represent Christ's purity. Peppermint and wintergreen flavoring was also added, it was thought, because the flavor is similar to the herb hyssop—a member of the mint family used in Old Testament times as part of purification rites.

American candy maker Paul Ghinelli is credited by the *Guinness Book of World Records* as having created the largest handmade candy canes—and he did so on three separate occasions. In 1998, he made a 16-foot-long candy cane, followed by a 36-foot version in 2000 and the mother of all candy canes—a 58-foot monster—in 2001.

Today, the candy cane has a special place in the hearts of the American public, and December 26 is known as "National Candy Cane Day."

DID YOU KNOW?

The only East Asian country to celebrate Christmas as a public holiday is South Korea.

In a Pickle?

This is one of those stories whose origins have a number of versions. And even though all are hard to verify, the tradition described here is one that is actually practiced.

According to one source, hanging a pickle on the Christmas tree is a German tradition that began as a way of teaching children to be observant. The story goes that a glass pickle was hidden in the decorated tree, and the first child in the family to spot the ornament was rewarded with an extra Christmas gift. In this version, it's not quite clear why the odd-man-out ornament is a pickle. But the answer to "why a pickle?" is quite clear in the second variation.

This tradition has the glass pickle as a symbol of how one prisoner of war ate a pickle to get out of a pickle, as it were. Apparently, some time during the American Civil War, between 1861 and 1865, a Bavarian man named John Lower was locked up in the Andersonville prison. Near death, having had nothing to eat, he convinced a guard to give him some food. The guard gave the prisoner a pickle from his lunch. It revived him beyond belief, he survived his incarceration, and when he was finally released, Lower developed the tradition of hiding a glass pickle in the Christmas tree, with the family member who first discovered it being blessed with good luck in the coming year.

Really!

DID YOU  KNOW?

Children in Syria have to wait for their Christmas presents until January 6. And when the gifts finally arrive, Santa has a most unusual helper. Legend in that country gives this honor to the smallest of the Wise Men's camels. In Finland, a goat made of straw and named Ukko is Santa's helper and is responsible for gift delivery to Finnish youngsters.

Advent Calendars

While it's not clear where the Advent calendar originated, some scholars believe it dates back to the early 20th century in Germany. Regardless, the clever idea is a wonderful way to help youngsters count down the days to Christmas.

Typically, a calendar made of cloth, wood or paper is hung in a prominent place in the family home. Twenty-five slots usually hold an ornament of some type, which the youngsters in the family take turns removing—one day at a time—and placing on the Christmas tree.

The concept of the Advent calendar offers endless possibilities. In recent years, chocolate Advent calendars provide a sweet treat for each day in the big countdown to Christmas.

SUNG TAN CHUK HA

in Korean

Other Seasonal Traditions

While Christmas celebrations dominate the media and retailers cater to all things Christmas, the months of November through January are also a time for people of other faiths to celebrate their traditions. Unfortunately, it's a sad reality of our time that tolerance for diverse celebrations and traditions, even at Christmastime—a time for peace on earth and goodwill to all—isn't always there.

But a closer look at traditions that might be unfamiliar will only serve to remove the mystery and enhance the magic of the season. So regardless whether you are Christian, Jew, Zoroastrian or atheist, if you're a connoisseur of human nature, I'm sure the stories and tidbits that follow will add substance to your personal seasonal journey.

NOT JUST CHRISTMAS

Hanukkah, Feast of the Dedication

Also known as the "Festival of Lights," Hanukkah has been a beloved celebration of the Jewish people since 164 BC. But to really understand the tradition of Hanukkah, you need to understand the story behind its origin.

It was 168 BC, and the political climate in Jerusalem was about to undergo considerable upheaval. A Syrian king named Antiochus Epiphanes was on the throne at the time. Also known as the "Mad King," Antiochus Epiphanes was renowned for his cruelty and ruled with an iron fist—unbending in his decisions

and, as is often the case with this kind of personality, unreasonable as well.

Wanting to secure his absolute power over the people of his rule, his first bit of business was to ensure that everyone not only looked to him as king but also worshipped him as a god. That was nothing short of blasphemy to the Hebrew people, who despite their differences of belief with their Syrian rulers, had managed to establish some semblance of a peaceful life for themselves in Jerusalem. And when they refused to bow down and worship Antiochus Epiphanes, their temple was vandalized, their altars were defiled, and even their scriptures were burned.

Mattathias, a Jewish high priest, could no longer tolerate the sacrilege, and when a Syrian soldier was in the process of sacrificing a pig on their altar, Mattathias raised his sword and killed the soldier. His five sons joined him in an effort to reclaim their temple, killing all the Syrian soldiers in attendance. No one in recent memory had defied a Syrian king so completely, and knowing their lives were in danger, Mattathias and his sons took refuge in the nearby mountains. Despite the fact that they were few in number and had no real weapons to speak of, the band of men, which grew bigger over time, came to be known as the "Maccabees," and they vowed to overthrow their Syrian oppressors. The fighting, which lasted for three long years, culminated in a final attack in December of 164 BC. That's when the Maccabees stormed Jerusalem, defeated the Syrian army and rededicated the temple.

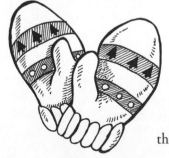

Today, Hanukkah—which in Hebrew literally means "dedication"—commemorates that rededication of the Jewish temple in Jerusalem and begins on the 25th of Kislev in the Hebrew calendar (November or December in the Gregorian calendar).

The Festival of Lights portion of Hanukkah is a remembrance of a miracle experienced by the Maccabees, who after cleansing the temple wanted to light the menorah. It is customary to have the flame—known as the "eternal flame"—lit continuously, but only enough oil could be found to last for a single day. Miraculously, despite the small amount of oil, the flame endured for eight days and nights, which was long enough for more oil to be obtained. To commemorate this miracle, the Festival of Lights continues for eight days and nights.

The menorah has changed somewhat over the years. Instead of lighting traditional clay vessels filled with olive oil, eight candles are used to represent the eight days and nights of the first miracle, and a central candle known as the *Shamash* or "servant" is used to light the other candles.

Although Hanukkah is a religious holiday, the practice of gift giving is a recent addition to the festivities and is likely the result of the fact that the Jewish tradition takes place so close to Christmas.

DID YOU  KNOW?

When visiting jolly old Saint Nicholas at Macy's New York City department store, each child only sits on his lap for an average of 37 seconds.

Bodhi Day or Rohatsu

The beginning of December is a sacred time for those of the Buddhist faith. Bodhi Day, or Rohatsu, is set aside as a time to revere Siddhartha Gautama. In 596 BC, Siddhartha Gautama was a religious student who, after six years of study, broke away from his group and sat under a pipal tree for eight days until, all of a sudden, everything made sense—he'd experienced an epiphany of sorts. Right there, under that pipal, Siddhartha

Gautama was believed to have achieved enlightenment. Simply put, this means he had succeeded in escaping the repeating cycle of reincarnation, which is birth, life, death and rebirth. Through this enlightenment, he developed the Four Noble Truths of the religion that came to be known as Buddhism, and Siddhartha Gautama was thereafter called Buddha. While the date isn't permanently fixed year after year, Bodhi Day is usually celebrated on December 8 or the Sunday prior to that date.

DID YOU KNOW?

Santa Claus was first featured in the 1903 movie *A Fantasy Actually Filmed in Northern Alaska*. Don't worry, nobody else knew that either!

The Ninth Month

Ramadan is a Muslim holiday that is often celebrated during the Christmas season. But anyone with Muslim friends and acquaintances will likely notice that Ramadan is not celebrated at the same time every year.

This is because Ramadan is considered a lunar holiday and takes place during the month of Ramadan—the ninth month of the Islamic or Hijri calendar. However, because the months of this calendar are shorter than those of the conventional calendar, averaging 29.53 days each, the Islamic calendar shifts from year to year compared to the Christian calendar.

As with most faith-based traditions, the festival of Ramadan commemorates a significant event in Islamic history. It is believed that the prophet Muhammad was sitting alone in the wilderness one Ramadan, when he first received the Koran in the form of a golden tablet from the angel

Gabriel. The angel instructed the prophet to read it carefully, as it contained the very essence of the Islamic faith.

Another event of significance to the tradition of Ramadan was the Battle of Badr, the first battle between the Arabian cities of Mecca and Medina. In that confrontation, the Muslims of Medina were victorious over the idol worshippers of Mecca.

For practicing Muslims, fasting during Ramadan is as essential as breathing. It is said to teach self-discipline and is a requirement for Muslims to "prepare for the suffering that Muslims may have to face in the course of obeying their God."

From the age of 12, Muslims who have reached puberty, are of sound mind, healthy and "not in a state of travel" are taught to abstain from eating or drinking anything whatsoever from sunrise to sunset. Women who are not menstruating or bleeding from childbirth are also expected to participate in the fasting ritual. Abstaining from sexual relations and a focused effort on prayer and meditation from sunrise to sunset each day during the 29 or 30 days of Ramadan are also components of this Muslim tradition.

The period of fasting ends with a feast, Eid-ul-Fitr, to signal the end of Ramadan and the start of the 10th month, known as Shawwal.

Zartusht-No-Diso

Practitioners of the ancient religion of Zoroastrianism believe they are "among those who renew the world...to make the world progress towards perfection." December 26 is when Zoroastrians celebrate Zartusht-no-diso in remembrance of the death anniversary of Zarathustra. Although this religion is so old that some scholars believe its founder, Zarathustra, lived as much as 6000 years before Plato, the tenets of that faith are still quite palatable today, and Zoroastrianism continues to have a solid following in India.

A Celebration of Human Rights

On December 10, 1948, the General Assembly of the United Nations signed the Universal Declaration of Human Rights. Consisting of 30 articles of belief, the document promotes dignity and equal rights for all people. Every year since 1948, December 10 has been known as "Human Rights Day." Typically, a theme is decided on and a focus on promoting education and awareness on that theme and all other issues of human rights are part of celebrations held in communities around the world.

DID YOU KNOW?

Santa Claus is called Joulupukki in Finland. Literally translated, the name means "Yule goat" or "Christmas goat." The name likely harkens back to a time when people dressed in goat hides called *nuuttipukkis* and traveled door to door eating all the Christmas leftovers.

Promoting Peace

Since 1997, the "1000 Lamp Mandala Ceremony" has been held every December 10 in an effort to promote world peace. The date is significant for several reasons. Initiated by Thubten Dorje Lakha Rinpoche, the Lhama of Bantag East Tibet, the focus of the 1000 Lamp Mandala Ceremony is to promote peace in the world, so hosting it on the same day as Human Rights Day is a good fit. December 10, 1997, was also the day Lhama Dhondrug, the 14th Dalai Lama of Tibet, received the Nobel Peace Prize.

Kwanzaa

Kwanzaa is a celebration of family values that emphasizes community responsibility and also focuses on self-improvement. This might sound like values that echo those of Christmas. But even though the annual African American tradition of Kwanzaa runs over the Christmas season, from December 26 to January 1, those who practice it are quick to point out it's neither meant to affirm nor replace the Christian celebration.

The word *kwanzaa* is a Kiswahili word that means "first fruits of the harvest." The practice of Kwanzaa and its annual cultural festivities were developed in 1966 by a University of California professor of Nigerian birth named Dr. Maulana Karenga. His goal wasn't to create another religion, nor establish a political movement. Instead, Kwanzaa was meant to provide a conscious opportunity for African Americans to reaffirm their value as people and to remember their ancestors and their culture. Since the days between Christmas and New Year were already set aside for holiday festivities, he decided that strategically placing Kwanzaa at that time would make it accessible to many people who already may have had time off work.

Simply put, a main focus is assigned to each of the seven days of Kwanzaa and are known as *Nguzo Saba* or the "Seven Guiding Principles":

- *Umoja* (unity) focuses on family and community togetherness;

- *Kujichagulia* (self-determination) stresses making decisions that are in the best interest of all;

- *Ujima* (collective work and responsibility) reminds practitioners of their obligation to the past, present and future, and that each individual has a role to play in the community, society and the world;

- *Ujamaa* (cooperative economics) emphasizes the idea of strength in numbers when it comes to economic success;

- *Nia* (purpose) encourages inner reflection and goal setting that benefits the community as well as the individual;

🔔 *Kuumba* (creativity) highlights the importance of creativity in building community;

🔔 *Imani* (faith) encourages practitioners to believe in themselves and use their abilities for the greater good of humankind in general.

Today, just four decades since its inception, Kwanzaa is practiced by 18 million people around the world.

DID YOU  KNOW?

Forget the traditional mail route—kids in England have a rather strange way of sending their wish list to Santa. After they write out their lists, they throw them into the fireplace to burn, and the smoke carries their wishes to Santa.

Omisoka

The two most important days in the Japanese tradition are New Year's Eve and New Year's Day. This is because, for the Japanese, these days signify the ending of one year and the beginning of another. Cleaning is the order of the day for most Japanese households to prepare to welcome in the new year with everything—including people's minds and bodies—in a fresh, clean state, all ready for the new beginning that New Year's Day signifies.

Rebirth of the Sun

Imagine this—you're gathered together with your family enjoying watermelon and pomegranates, laughing over old stories and reading poetry. Eventually you might move outside and build a roaring bonfire. Sound wonderful? These activities are just part of the

traditional Shab-e Yalda Festival—the birthday or rebirth of the sun. This ancient festival, which typically takes place on the day of the winter solstice, has Iranian Persian roots, but evolved into a festival now celebrated by a variety of cultures and religions. Each of the activities described above occurs for a reason. For example, the bonfire is lit to burn all night to defeat the forces of Ahriman, an ancient demon that compares with the Christian Satan.

NADOLIG LLAWEN
in Welsh

New Year's Traditions

If you thought that Christmas had cornered the market when it came to unique traditions, you were mistaken.

The turn of the calendar year has typically meant much more than just another day and another year. To tell you the truth, New Year's Eve has always left me cold with worry as I looked out into a vast unknown. Somehow, page one of any adventure is a little anxiety-provoking for me. It seems I'm not alone.

Traditions around the world developed over time to ensure the coming year would be one bestowing health, happiness and prosperity to all. And of course, a rip-roaring party never hurt anyone! So in the immortal words of Alfred Lord Tennyson, as we count down to the next new year to cross our path, may we join in saying:

☞

Ring out the old, ring in the new,
Ring happy bells across the snow;
The year is going, let him go;
Ring out the false, ring in the new.

START THE YEAR OFF RIGHT

Reveillon

Brazilians "awaken" the New Year with a custom they call "Reveillon," a derivative of the French word *reveiller*. In direct opposition to the more formal, religious Christmas celebrations, Brazilians have adopted an assortment of European, African and American traditions and party quite heartily when welcoming in the new year. Reflecting on the devout nature of a considerably Catholic and Christian population, it may be surprising to some that Reveillon, an all-day, all-night festival, is held each year in Rio de Janeiro and began as a ceremony honoring the African goddess of the sea, Iemanja. But the African traditions of Umbanda and Candomble are firmly entrenched in Brazilian

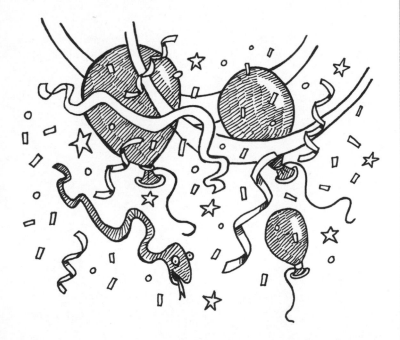

life, and along with their adoption by
that country, have evolved
through the years. Umbana, for
example, is a culmination of
Congolese, Angolan,
Yoruban, Roman Catholic,
spiritualist, Kardecis and
indigenous Brazilian spiritual traditions.
And even for devout Catholics, Reveillon is a
celebration not to be missed!

During the more formal portion of the celebration, participants
dressed primarily in white to signify prosperity, peace and good
luck, make their way to the shores of one of Rio's many beaches
carrying flowers with them as an offering to the sea. At nightfall, white candles are lit and placed in a horseshoe shape in the
sand as drums sound in the background. Legend has it that participants dance, sing and "convulse" as Iemanja actually enters
their bodies.

The leader of the ceremony, known as the "celebrant," conducts
a ritual cleansing that bears some similarity to baptism, dipping
participants' heads into the water for those who request it.

The party portion of Reveillon is no less elaborate than the
spiritual celebration. Everyone dresses up for the occasion, and
along with the citywide shindig Rio de Janeiro puts on each
year, smaller, more intimate events are also common in hotels
and private homes across the country. For women who are
able, fancy ball gowns and elaborate headdresses are the attire
of the day. For the men, it's a traditional black tie event. The
music continues until dawn, but just before the clock strikes
12:00 AM the crowd is typically silent, waiting for the countdown to begin.

And at the stroke of midnight, if a Brazilian woman wants to
ensure a lucky love life for the coming year, it is customary for

her to exchange a New Year's greeting with three men before she speaks to another woman. The same holds true, in reverse of course, for the men.

One of Brazil's most well-loved festivals is Carnival. Although this event, characterized by costume balls, numerous parades and fancy parties, doesn't begin until four days prior to the start of Lent, which is several months later, Reveillon is considered the beginning of Carnival.

DID YOU  KNOW?

Most North Americans are familiar with the American New Year's tradition of the Rose Bowl football game, but did you know that for several years—from 1897 to 1916—chariot racing replaced football as the big New Year's event.

Hogmanay

Known as Hogmanay, the Scottish tradition of welcoming in the New Year is considered the most important midwinter holiday in Scotland, much more important than Christmas. Its popularity so outraged the Church that it was formally denounced in church records.

As for the literal meaning of the word Hogmanay, linguists appear to be uncertain. While one school suggests it evolved from the French word *aguillaneuf*, meaning "New Year's gift," another believes it comes from the Spanish word *aguilnaldo*,

which, depending on your preference, means "Christmas tip," "New Year's gift" or "Christmas carol." There are countless other theories about the origin of the word, but most are rejected by academics. Regardless, the celebration typically begins December 31 and can continue to January 2.

Several customs stem directly from Hogmanay, beginning with the "first footer." There are, it seems, an endless number of superstitions surrounding the first footer in Scottish folklore. Hair color, sex, age and the token gift presented by the first person to step over your threshold after midnight on New Year's Eve are all symbolic and signal the kind of luck you're likely to have in the coming year. Depending on the particular beliefs you adhere to, a tall, dark and handsome man brings the best luck to your home provided, of course, that he isn't flat-footed. A flat-footed visitor is believed to bring bad luck. And while some Scots believe a fair or red-headed stranger is a bad sign for the future, others disagree. If a first footer hands you a gift of salt or a "sprig of greenery" you will be blessed by good luck, and you should return the kind gesture with food and drink.

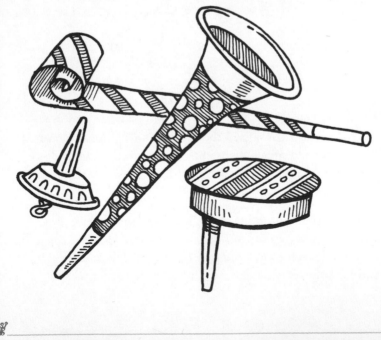

Similarly, the first person you meet while walking down the road is believed to be a sign of your future fortune. Meeting a child is considered lucky, but if you meet a gravedigger, you might not want to put off that long overdue appointment with your family doctor any longer.

Another interesting custom that takes place during Hogmanay is the "fireball swing," an annual event that takes place in Stonehaven, Kincardineshire. It involves a group of people making a 3-foot-wide ball of chicken wire wrapped in tar, paper and other flammable material, which is secured to a 6-foot length of wire or chain and lit on fire. Then a "swinger" swings the ball around his or her head while walking from the Stonehaven harbor to the "Sheriff court" and back. It appears this custom is all for the flaming effect, kind of like modern-day fireworks, rather than to predict or create good or bad luck.

DID YOU KNOW?

Lifting the plum pudding from the pot gets a lot more than a round of applause in Newfoundland; it gets a round of gunfire, according to an old tradition of "blowing the pudding."

Chinese New Year

Everything about celebrating Chinese New Year is unique, beginning with the date it's celebrated on. While most of the world ushers in the New Year on January 1, or relatively soon thereafter, celebrations in China are determined by the Chinese calendar and usually fall between January 21 and February 21. Because the Chinese calendar is lunisolar, celebrations begin with the new moon and conclude 15 days later with a full moon.

While Chinese New Year celebrations outside China may adopt local customs, some traditions continue in the same manner they've been practiced for thousands of years. Fire is an important component of these celebrations. Firecrackers are lit in an effort to chase away evil spirits and bring good fortune. It was also hoped the noisemakers would wake the gods and guardian spirits, bringing good health and prosperity.

The lion is considered a holy animal and is another important symbol in Chinese culture. Thought to be associated with "courage, stability and superiority," the lion is the focal point of the Lion Dance that is performed during the Lantern Festival, which takes place on the 15th day of the New Year and symbolizes the end of Chinese New Year celebrations. According to tradition, if the dance is done correctly, it will bring happiness and luck and scare evil away.

DID YOU  **KNOW?**

Charles Dickens set the price of his 1843 novel, *A Christmas Carol*, at a mere five shillings. That's because he thought it so important a read, he wanted everyone to be able to afford a copy.

MILAD MAJID
in Arabic

Christmas News
from Around
the World

Have you ever noticed how the evening news, good or bad, seems to have a greater impact during the Christmas season?

We rejoice at the good news stories with far more exuberance than at other times of the year, and tragedy seems so much more profound. After all, it's Christmas. A season of peace and happiness and goodwill to all people! Life should be good.

What follows are a few unique stories that made news if for no other reason than they had to do with Christmas.

STRANGE BUT TRUE

Christmas-Lover Extraordinaire

This one comes from Scotland's national newspaper, the *Scotsman*. A story dated November 29, 2005, heralds 45-year-old Andy Park—otherwise known as Mr. Christmas, if you please—and his dedication to celebrating the Christmas season year round. For 12 years, the Scottish bro has been consuming 25 Brussels' sprouts, along with a roast turkey dinner befitting the most particular Christmas diner's palate, every day—that's *every day*—for 12 years now. Apparently, he just can't get enough Christmas in his life and he uses food to prove it, consuming one turkey, 20 mince pies and six roast potatoes daily. Over the years, he's also downed 4380 bottles each of champagne and sherry, as well as 5000 bottles of wine. Along with the food and spirits, he's a pretty good gift giver, too. And in the end, this man—who makes his living as an electrician—estimates he's spent about £250,000 on his Christmas-loving lifestyle over the last 12 years—something he hopes to continue to do for many years to come.

DID YOU KNOW?

Six publishers rejected the book *The Christmas Box* before one took a chance on publishing it. Of course, it went on to be a runaway bestseller, a made-for-TV movie and catapulted its author onto the *New York Times* bestseller list.

Politically Correct?

The trend these days is to nix the idea of saying "Merry Christmas" in favor of something more inclusive, such as "Happy Holidays." But the move to change the city and county signs to the new slogan met with disapproval among the folks in Denver, Colorado, back in 2004. *FOX News* reported that the mayor at the time, John Hickenlooper, got the message from his constituents loud and clear and decided the "Merry Christmas" signs should stay.

Still, the war over politically correct seasonal language rages on. Good old California Governor Arnold Schwarzenegger made the news when he decided to call that state's "holiday tree" a "Christmas tree" during the 2004 lighting ceremony. *ABC News* reported a dispute over the renaming of the "holiday tree" on Capitol Hill to the "Christmas tree" in November 2005. And that same year in Boston, the reverse caused a commotion when officials in that city tried to rename their Christmas tree the "holiday tree."

These stories are by no means unique. The issue of inclusive holiday language seems to pop up every year in some context or other. So if you ever wondered about the true power of words, this should settle the matter. The pen truly seems to be more powerful than the sword!

DID YOU  KNOW?

A sequoia tree named the "General Grant Tree" is located in Kings Canyon National Park in California and was named America's "National Christmas Tree" in 1926. It is over 267 feet tall, more than 40 feet in diameter and is estimated to be 1500 to 2000 years old.

Statistics Galore

It seems there's a study for just about everything under the sun, including one on the Christmas card–giving practices of the British.

According to a November 2002 report from the British Heart Foundation, 13 percent of the folks in the south of Britain didn't send any cards that year, giving the folks in the north something to brag about, since only seven percent of them were guilty of the same Scrooge-like crime against seasonal festivities. At the same time, the folks down south sent more char-ity Christmas cards than their northern partners—50 percent compared with 37 percent. And apparently, cards featur-ing our friend the Christmas robin, "idyllic, homely scenes" and religious or traditional illustrations are favored for giving.

So get your pen ready, pick up all the stamps you need, and gear yourself up for a Christmas card extravaganza this year, lest you find yourself being compared with Scrooge!

Peace in a War Zone

It's the stuff of urban legend, you might think. But in the midst of the ravages of war, at a time when your enemy still had a face and you looked into their eyes when engaged in hand-to-hand combat, a Christmas miracle occurred.

The year was 1914 and World War I was well underway. But as Christmas approached, the mood softened slightly until the unthinkable happened—a truce was called on this most holy of holidays in the Christian calendar. British, German, French and Belgian troops gathered in what is commonly referred to as

"No Man's Land"—the territory between enemy trenches—
to celebrate the day with a friendly game of football and a gift
exchange. And though not the only instance of its kind, what
has come to be known as the "Christmas Truce" shines to this
day as an example of hope in what seems like a hopeless
situation.

DID YOU  KNOW?

Sir Issac Newton (1642), Humphrey Bogart (1899), Little
Richard (1932) and Sissy Spacek (1949) all have one thing in
common. They were all born on Christmas Day.

Santa Mania

All hail real-bearded Santas!

The Amalgamated Order of Real Bearded Santas (AORBS) made history in July 2006 with their first-ever annual convention. But wait—you say you've never heard of the group before? Well, where exactly have you been, anyway?

The AORBS started out in August 1994, when a group of 10 Santas were preparing for a television commercial for OTTO, a German mail-order company. The group, who were all real-bearded Santas by the way, got to talking and thought it would be a grand idea to get together regularly. They picked the date—the third Sunday of January 1995. After all, the holiday rush would have subsided by then and they'd get a chance to reminisce over their most recent Christmas memories of playing Santa for the hundreds of youngsters that had sat on their lap that year.

By 1997, the meeting had become an annual event and the original gathering of 10 Santas had grown to include many more. By April 2006, more than 800 "real-bearded" Santas from across the U.S., Australia, New Zealand, Europe, the Middle East and Canada counted themselves among the group.

The inaugural Amalgamated Order of Real Bearded Santas International Convention was held in Branson, Missouri, in July 2006. Three hundred real-bearded Santas, as well as numerous Mrs. Santas and Santa's helpers, gathered for the event. Workshop topics for the four-day convention included everything from "Dealing with Special-Needs Children" and "Storytelling" to "Dealing with the Male Peacock: How to Live with Santa" (delivered by one Mrs. Santa to her fellow colleagues), "Care and Feeding of Santa's Beard" and "Keeping Christ as the Center of our Christmas."

DID YOU KNOW?

The original 10 members of the Amalgamated Order of Real Bearded Santas were Joe Crozier, Harry Frazier, Tom Hartsfield, Bob Kokol, Joe Leavitt, Jim Lewis, Ed Murphy, Leonard Ray, Frank Turner and Jay Wright.

Santa Stats

Based on the survey responses of 294 members of the AORBS, the average Santa is 59.25 years old, is 69.81 inches in height and weighs in at 257.24 pounds. He's been married about 24.36 years, has 2.74 children, 3.43 grandchildren and 0.27 great-grandchildren. Here are a few more particulars:

- The average Santa has been at the job for 11.62 years.

- He's had a beard for 8.78 years.

- One hundred fifty-eight of the respondents had blue eyes, 64 had brown eyes, 54 had hazel eyes and 18 had green eyes.

- Fifty-five percent or 162 had served in some part of the military: 44 were in the air force, 51 in the army, three in the Coast Guard, 16 were in the marines, four were in the National Guard and 43 were in the navy.

- A total of 88.43 percent of the respondents were married.

- Eighty-one Santas first donned a red suit because they were asked to by their families, 64 were asked by their co-workers, and 50 just decided they liked what they saw and jumped on board.

- Santas are considerably educated, too. Of the respondents, 41 had an Associated Arts degree, 65 had a Bachelor of Arts degree, 33 had a Masters degree, five had a PhD and two were doctors.

It may surprise you that none of the real-bearded Santas traveled via reindeer. Instead, two had 18-wheelers, five had a hybrid vehicle, 50 drove vans, 66 had SUVs, 88 drove sedans or compact cars and 91 drove pickup trucks. A total of 13.7 percent rode a motorcycle in addition to their main vehicles.

Being practicing Santas, it's a cinch that the favorite movies of the real-bearded Santa survey participants are Christmas movies: 17.96 percent said it was *It's a Wonderful Life*, 21.35 percent voted for *Santa Clause*, and 54.57 percent said their favorite movie was *Miracle on 34th Street*.

🔔 Rudolph is easily the most popular reindeer when it comes to the AORBS survey—63.4 percent voted him as their favorite.

🔔 *The Night Before Christmas* was voted as the favorite book of 75.9 percent of those taking the survey.

🔔 Overall, members of the AORBS spend 27.85 days in their red suits. They see an average of 200 kids per day and about 3593.20 youngsters in a season.

🔔 Oh, and in case you were wondering, Santa's favorite cookie is chocolate chip, according to 129 of survey respondents. Another 59 preferred oatmeal raisin, 28 preferred peanut butter, 25 preferred sugar cookies and eight preferred Oreos.

DID YOU KNOW?

The French call eggnog *lait de poule*, which directly translated means "chicken's milk."

Christmas at the Museum

Chicago's Museum of Science and Industry might be very well known for housing the only U-505 German submarine in existence, but for Christmas lovers around the world it also has another claim to fame. From mid-November to January 7, the museum celebrates Christmas—along with other seasonal holidays such as Hanukkah, Kwanzaa and Chinese New Year—with an all-out display of more than 50 Christmas trees. The exhibit is known as the "Annual Christmas Around the World and Holidays of Light," and the trees are each decorated to feature a different ethnic tradition. The museum also hosts a series of performances highlighting traditional ethnic stories, displays and performances.

VESELÉ VIANOCE
in Slovak

Beyond Unique

Let's face it. Some Christmas traditions are just a little more unique than others. In fact, it could be argued that some might be considered downright weird.

Here are a few such traditions that might just leave you scratching your head in wonder.

ONE-OF-A-KIND CUSTOMS

Horsing Around

Imagine this—skulking around under a *brethyn rhawn*, a horse-hair sheet, with a horse's skull in hand. Apparently, the old Welsh tradition called *Mair Lwyd* features just such a scoundrel who wanders about alongside a group of mummers. And if he or she nips you with the horse's skull, you are expected to dole out some cash.

DID YOU KNOW?

The tradition of holding Midnight Mass on Christmas Eve comes from the belief that the Christ child was born at exactly midnight.

Mother's Day in December

Mothers in Yugoslavia get to look forward to a rather unique take on the whole concept of Mother's Day. Forget about getting gifts of adornment, in that country you have to pay your way out of bondage.

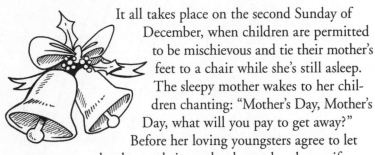

It all takes place on the second Sunday of December, when children are permitted to be mischievous and tie their mother's feet to a chair while she's still asleep. The sleepy mother wakes to her children chanting: "Mother's Day, Mother's Day, what will you pay to get away?" Before her loving youngsters agree to let her loose, their mother has to hand out gifts. And before you thank your lucky stars that you're a father and spared this treatment, think again. Yugoslavian fathers get their turn at being thusly tormented the following Sunday.

Grow Your Own Decorations

The Lebanese take the task of decorating a nativity scene to an entirely new level. In that country, chickpeas, wheat grains, beans and lentils are planted in cotton wool two weeks before Christmas. These seeds are watered daily and by Christmas are well sprouted. These shoots are then used as part of the manger scene.

The Touch of Peace

Christian families in Iraq have developed a rather unique tradition. On Christmas Eve, parents hold lighted candles while their children read the story of the Nativity. This is often done in the family courtyard, but if not, they all then venture outdoors and sing a psalm around a bonfire of dried thorns. The family will be blessed with good luck in the coming year if the thorns burn to ash. When the fire has burned down, everyone jumps over the ashes three times and makes a wish.

A similar, though lengthier ceremony is conducted at church on Christmas Day, complete with the bonfire and all. The bishop then leads a procession throughout the church and finishes off by blessing one member of the congregation by touching someone with his hand. That person then passes the touch to the next person and so on until all those in the church have received the "Touch of Peace."

Roller-Skating Revelry

Folks in Caracas, the capital city of Venezuela, have developed a rather unique way of getting to church on Christmas morning. Apparently, streets there are closed to vehicle traffic until 8:00 AM, so that anyone who can will roller-skate their way to morning mass. Adding to this strange tradition is the practice of young children tying a string to their big toe before bed on Christmas Eve and hanging the string out the window. In the morning they will most assuredly wake to find roller skates tied to the string.

Brooms and Bladders

Here's one that's definitely weird. In fact, this ancient custom, hailing from the town of Laupen, Switzerland, is so bizarre that the town priest successfully lobbied to have it moved from its original celebratory date of Christmas Eve to New Year's Eve. The tradition goes something like this. Three groups of young boys meet on the hill at the local castle and proceed down to the village. Each group carries one of three items: large swinging bells, bunches of juniper attached to the end of long, broomstick-type poles and pigs' bladders filled with air. The lads with the bells ring them loudly and constantly. The boys with the juniper bunches are called "broom men," and they swing their poles back and forth as they walk. And the guys with the pigs' bladders filled with air—well, they squeeze them, producing a sound that I'll leave to your imagination. In any case, these youngsters stop from time to time at people's homes and recite a rhyme or two bidding farewell to the old year and welcoming in the new. And once they finally make it to the village, these young lads proceed to playfully "beat" onlookers, especially young ladies, until their weapons are in pieces. It's no wonder the poor parish priest didn't see this as a fitting event for Christmas Eve!

DID YOU  KNOW?

The King of Rock and Roll might be dead, but Elvis Presley's beloved Graceland is still decorated to the hilt every Christmas to honor the tradition he began.

KELLEMES KARACSONYI UNNEPEKET
in Hungarian

Ho Ho Ho!

What would a holiday be without a few seasonal jokes?
Here are a few about Christmas.

CHRISTMAS JOKES

Q: Why are Christmas trees like bad knitters?
A: They both drop their needles!

Q: What did the bald man say when he got a comb for Christmas?
A: Thanks, I'll never part with it!

Q: What do snowmen eat for lunch?
A: Icebergers!

Q: Why does Santa have three gardens?
A: So he can ho-ho-ho!

Q: If Santa Claus and Mrs. Claus had a child, what would he be called?
A: A subordinate Claus.

Q: What do elves learn in school?
A: The elf-abet!

Q: Why is Christmas just like a day at the office?
A: You do all the work, and the fat guy in the suit gets all the credit.

Q: Why was Santa's little helper depressed?
A: Because he had low elf esteem!

Q: What do you get if you deep-fry Santa Claus?
A: Crisp Kringle.

Modern Christmas at its Best

As a little girl climbs onto Santa's lap, Santa asks the usual: "And what would you like for Christmas?" The child stares at him open-mouthed and horrified for a minute, then gasps: "But Santa, didn't you get my e-mail?"

ABOUT THE ILLUSTRATOR

Roger Garcia

Roger Garcia lived in El Salvador until he was seven years old, when his parents moved him to North America. Because of the language barrier, he had to find a way to communicate with other kids. That's when he discovered the art of tracing. It wasn't long before he mastered this highly skilled technique, and by age 14 he was drawing cartoons for a weekly newspaper. He taught himself to paint and sculpt, and then in high school and college, Roger skipped class to hide in the art room all day in order to further explore his talent.

ABOUT THE AUTHOR

Lisa Wojna

Lisa Wojna, author of several other non-fiction books, has worked in the community newspaper industry as a writer and journalist. She has traveled all over North America and even to the wilds of Africa. Although writing and photography have been a central part of her life for as long as she can remember, it's the people behind every story that are her motivation and give her the most fulfillment.